Veteran journalist Tim Stafford ~~do best: reports on the world of~~ ~~ticism nor naïveté but with clari~~ ~~remarkable achievement.~~

—Eugene H. Peterson, Professor Emeritus of Spiritual Theology, Regent College, Vancouver, B.C.

Tim has taken one of the most important and fascinating topics in the world and written about it with honesty, faith, and grace. His look at miracles through history and across cultures is full of wisdom and longing. This book—if not actually miraculous itself—is at least providential.

—John Ortberg, senior pastor of Menlo Park Presbyterian Church and author of *Who Is This Man?*

When I started reading this fine book, I was what Tim Stafford labels a "Semi-Believing Doubter" on the subject of present-day miracles. I no longer wear that label. *Miracles* is a gripping—and convincing—account of how God continues to astonish us with signs of a power that will someday come into its fullness!

—Richard J. Mouw, PhD, President and Professor of Christian Philosophy, Fuller Theological Seminary

There are journalists of miracles and there are guides to miracles. Tim Stafford is a sure guide to skeptics and believers alike, showing how contemporary Christians not only live in the miraculous stories of the Bible but also wrestle with what seems to be God's silence in these same pages.

—Amos Yong, J. Rodman Williams Professor of Theology, Regent University School of Divinity

Do you want to believe in miracles but have been put off either by Christians who insist that every problem should be solved by a miracle, or by the skepticism of God's miraculous intervention in human experience? Then this is your book! As a journalist, Stafford squarely faces and differentiates between actual occurrences of miracles and disappointing non-occurrences; as a Christian, he makes a conscious effort to be faithful to God's revelation in Scripture. The result is a book that will instruct you on how to think biblically about issues relating to miracles. The summary statements in the last two chapters alone are worth the price of the book.

—Ajith Fernando, Teaching Director,
Youth for Christ, Sri Lanka

Tim Stafford puts the right person at the center of miracle stories: not the charismatic leader through whom miracles come, nor the person who is healed, but God himself. This book will help you see genuine miracles as part of God's way of telling his own story, and will teach you to listen for what God is saying through them.

—David Neff, Editor in Chief, *Christianity Today*

Tim Stafford dives headfirst into this investigation of those special events we call miracles—signs and wonders that demonstrate God's supernatural power. Probing, clarifying, and speaking to skeptics and believers alike, Stafford is thoroughly convincing as he digs deep to comment on biblical and contemporary examples.

—Luci Shaw, author, *Breath for the Bones,*
What the Light Was Like

Miracles

A Journalist Looks at Modern Day
Experiences *of* God's Power

TIM STAFFORD

BETHANY HOUSE PUBLISHERS
a division of Baker Publishing Group
Minneapolis, Minnesota

Published by Bethany House Publishers
11400 Hampshire Avenue South
Bloomington, Minnesota 55438
www.bethanyhouse.com

Bethany House Publishers is a division of
Baker Publishing Group, Grand Rapids, Michigan

Printed in the United States of America

Library of Congress Cataloging-in-Publication Data
Stafford, Tim
    Miracles : a journalist looks at modern day experiences of God's power /
Tim Stafford.
        p.   cm.
    Summary: "A journalist explores claims of modern-day miracles to better understand how God is working in the world today"—Provided by publishers.
    ISBN 978-0-7642-0937-6 (pbk. : alk. paper)
    1. Miracles. I. Title.
BT97.3.S725 2012
231.7′3—dc23   2012004896

Cover design by Gearbox/Christopher Gilbert

Author is represented by Books & Such Literary Agency

12   13   14   15   16   17   18   7   6   5   4   3   2   1

Contents

Foreword

I am a journalist. For more than thirty years I have written for magazines covering the evangelical Christian church around the world.

As a journalist, I am not an expert in anything—not medicine, theology, or philosophy. What journalism gives me is wide exposure. I talk in depth to church leaders and scholars. I visit places that others don't go, and when I'm there I interview all kinds of people nonstop. I read widely. I attend events where I stop people during breaks and ask questions. I don't talk only to people I agree with; I interview people who are uncomfortably different from me.

I rarely go places to speak or teach. Rather, I go to listen and watch and ask questions. I try to keep my opinions from interfering with my chance to hear what other people believe. I'm there as a witness on behalf of others. People read what I write in order to gain a fair-minded understanding of an event, a personality, or a subject, so that they can make up their own minds.

I am committed to Jesus Christ and I believe the Bible. But beyond that, I don't start with an ideology or theology that requires me to interpret miracles in one particular way. I listen and try to make fair judgments.

We live in a time when the Pentecostal movement is dramatically changing the global church and its understanding of miracles. In many places around the world, miracles have moved to center stage. Wonderful events are reported, but so are alarming concerns. Some consider the church out of balance; others see it as reclaiming vital territory, thriving because it experiences the power of the Holy Spirit just as the early church did.

In writing about miracles, I'm dealing with a subject so big and broad that it's impossible to know everything. I can't visit every miracle-seeking ministry. I can't comprehensively cover every country where miracles are reported. (Indonesia? China? North Africa?) I can't begin to track down and evaluate every miracle reported in my hometown, let alone my state or my country or the world.

So I've taken a more personal approach, starting in my own church, where a dramatic story unfolded in front of me. I've gone on to describe miraculous claims I've encountered personally around the world. I've drawn together information from my research, including the Bible and church history.

For many people, miracles are not a question of theology but a matter of hope and desperation. Their understanding of what to expect shapes the way they think and live as Christians. It shapes the way they reach out to unbelieving neighbors and co-workers. It affects how they respond to trials and sickness. It greatly shapes how they think about God.

I hope this book will help you to think clearly and live biblically as you ponder what God is doing in the world today—and in your life.

Acknowledgments

I want to acknowledge friends who have helped me by reading and commenting on this book in various stages: Dean and Mindy Anderson, Chase Stafford, Robert Digitale, Harold Fickett, David Graham, Mike Griffin, Paul Gullixson, Peter Lundstrom, Fred Prudek, and Philip Yancey. I'm grateful for their suggestions, even those I did not follow.

1

A Real Miracle

Jeff Moore was a high school student in my church, a dark-haired, good-looking teenager, with paper-white skin and a slight build. He was well liked, polite, quiet but friendly. He never drew attention to himself or his problem.

Jeff had lost the use of his feet—they hurt so much that they would no longer carry his weight. He came to church in a wheelchair.

I didn't know Jeff or his family then, but I often saw them at morning worship. I attend a Presbyterian church with about six hundred members. It is a warm, Bible-believing, multigenerational church that is a little traditional but tries to be flexible. We sing hymns with an organ, but we also try to bridge the gap between generations by using contemporary songs with a band. Jeff's mother, Sheri, was one of a handful of worship leaders very visibly singing in the choir at the front of the church.

Jeff was visible because he was the only young person in a wheelchair. Every week his father wheeled him into church.

It could not have been easy to come to church that way, and their faces showed the strain, I thought. Yet Jeff was always present with his parents and his two younger brothers.

It made me sad to see this healthy young man so crippled. It brought mystification, too. I had never heard of a young person whose feet hurt so much he couldn't walk. Why couldn't the doctors figure it out? Somebody told me his case baffled them.

Then one Sunday morning, our pastor announced that Jeff's mother had something to share. Sheri stepped out of the choir and quietly said that Jeff had been healed. He had gone to a service at a church in another city, several hours away, and after healing prayer, he stepped out of his wheelchair. His pain was completely gone. He could walk. He could run. God had healed him, his mother said.

I heard several spontaneous expressions of praise—two or three exclamations of "Praise the Lord!" Later in the service, our pastor prayed and thanked God for what he had done for Jeff. But truthfully, the response was restrained. No whooping. No delirious thanks. And not a lot of buzz afterward. Maybe—and here I might be projecting my own feelings—there was some uncertainty as to how we should react.

I heard that Jeff's family was disappointed by the response. They had been bubbling over with joy, but they weren't met with the same emotions.

Why the restraint? I'm guessing at what others felt, because there wasn't any public discussion. I know what I felt, and I suspect it was typical.

I was very glad at Jeff's news, but I was hesitant to put too much weight on it. I didn't know what had caused Jeff's problem, but it seemed possible it was psychosomatic. The mind is a very tricky thing. What if we whooped it up over a miracle and then discovered that the problem came back days or weeks later? That wouldn't put God in a very good light. It wouldn't build anybody's faith.

I also worried about Jeff being disappointed. Sometimes people want so much for God to heal them that they convince themselves he has done so. But the problem doesn't really disappear. It comes back, and eventually the hurting person has to face reality—no miracle. Then he or she is left wondering why God put them through such high hopes and disappointment.

I witnessed this in college. At a Christian conference, one of my fellow students came to believe that God wanted to heal his poor eyesight. He stood and dramatically announced his conviction, hurling his glasses across the room. Later he had to retrieve them because his eyes were as bad as ever. (Fortunately, the glasses had not broken.)

I've seen the same thing with people plagued by chronic health issues or mental health struggles. They become convinced God has healed them, and tell others so, expecting everybody to praise God—until it's undeniable they are not healed.

As it turned out, those fears were misplaced in Jeff's case. Months later he was bouncing around like any other young man, utterly pain-free. He really was healed.

What does that say about those of us who hesitated? Was it a judgment on our lack of faith?

I wasn't very happy when I heard the reaction from the pastor at the church where Jeff was healed. He told his congregation about Jeff's healing with great jubilation—as he should have. Then he added, with equal jubilation, "A Presbyterian church in the Bay Area had its faith rocked!" and his congregation roared.

The implication seemed to be that stodgy Presbyterians had a few lessons to learn, as though miracles were a contest, with winning churches and losing churches.

That stuck in my craw a bit. But I had to admit I was envious of the pastor's self-assurance. I look to see God answer my prayers, but I'm never sure what God's answer will be. Is this a lack of faith? That's one of the questions I want to probe in this book.

In my sixty years, I have seen many people who prayed fervently and *didn't* see healing. How should I respond to that?

I long to see God's life in the world. I want to know where he is at work. I want to cooperate with him in the way he chooses to operate. I want to walk by his side, working with him. But I want it to be real—not hyped-up fantasy faith.

Nearly three years after Jeff's healing, I decided I needed to talk to him. Jeff's story had stayed in my mind. Why couldn't a Christian congregation—*my* congregation—celebrate such a wonderful healing with heart and soul? Why had Jeff received such a muted and mixed response?

Also, I wanted to know exactly what had happened to Jeff and his family. Had the healing been complete? In the years since, had pain returned?

I found Jeff's number in the church directory, called him up, and explained that I would like to hear his story. Jeff's voice over the phone was hesitant. He said he wasn't sure. I didn't press him, I just emphasized how much I would like to hear about what had happened to him, and asked him to think it over.

After I hung up, I wondered. Was there something embarrassing that he didn't want to share? Had pain come back to his feet? I hadn't seen him at church lately; it could be because we attended different services, but it could be something more troubling.

I had to leave several messages before I reached him again, and this made me wonder even more. But when I finally got through, Jeff agreed to talk.

I met him at a local coffee shop and almost didn't recognize him. I remembered him as slight and pale, but he had become tanned and strong.

His manner struck me even more. Jeff isn't a talker. He didn't volunteer details about his healing. Truthfully, he wasn't eager to talk about anything that far in the past. He had moved on, and that actually made his story more believable. Jeff was not selling anything. There wasn't a trace of hype in his manner. He was a just-the-facts guy.

Apparently he had been that way even when he was disabled. From what he said, he hadn't worked himself into a fever, praying for healing of his damaged feet. On the contrary, after five years of constant medical interventions—five separate surgeries, countless doctors' appointments, acupuncture, physical therapy, orthotics—he had just wanted to be left alone.

The problem with his feet had snuck up on him gradually. The Moores were an active, adventurous family. They backpacked, they hiked, they took up some kind of outdoor activity virtually every weekend. When Jeff was nine or ten, he began to complain about his feet when the family went hiking. His parents thought it was his boots.

After a family trip to the county fair, Jeff complained that his feet were killing him. His parents thought nothing of it. Who doesn't have hurting feet after walking around the fair all day?

When he was thirteen, Jeff had an accident on his skateboard, but instead of healing, his foot stayed swollen. Eventually he went to the doctor, who told him he had broken something called a tarsal coalition. Jeff had flat feet, and to make up for the lack of flexibility in his feet, his body had fused together some of the bones. When Jeff fell off his skateboard, the "fusion" had broken, so the doctors put Jeff in a cast to allow the break to heal.

But the bones didn't heal, and the pain continued.

The surgeons cut open his foot and put in a titanium peg. The surgery worked as intended—his foot developed an arch—but after a long recuperation, Jeff still felt severe pain. Six months later they operated on the other foot, with the same result. Jeff described his story to me:

> I have a jar at home filled with all the screws they put in and later took out. In the last operation they cut open my calf and lengthened the muscle, slit my heel, slid it over, and tried to remake my foot. [This elaborate surgery required Jeff to spend six months in a cast, and then relearn how to walk with his altered foot.] They succeeded, in a way. They really did form perfect arches. I no longer had flat feet. But the pain was still there.
>
> I could walk a little, but the more walking I did the more it hurt, until it was unbearable.
>
> By the time I was seventeen I was done with it. They wanted to do another surgery, something drastic that would fuse my bones together. But after five surgeries and nothing different, I just gave up on it. I went for acupuncture and electrical stimulation, but they didn't help, either.
>
> I was trying to accept that I was always going to be in a wheelchair. My parents were broken up by it, I think. They never really gave up hoping that I could walk again. I have

an aunt whom I've never met, who gave money to a church that prayed for me every week. They sent me a card telling me that they had prayed for me. I thought it was kind of odd, to tell you the truth. Nobody else prayed for me, that I knew of, and I'm not sure how I would have felt about it if they had offered. I definitely did not believe that healing could happen.

I wasn't really mad about it. Some days I was fine, some days I was just irritable. I wanted to forget about change and deal with what was going to be my life.

By that time, Jeff was attending the local junior college, pulling his wheelchair out of the back of his classic Mustang and rolling himself in and out of classes. At an adaptive PE class, he struck up a friendship with another student named Leland, who was also in a wheelchair. Leland was older than Jeff and covered in tattoos. He had lost the use of his legs years before. A very friendly guy, Leland invited Jeff to join a wheelchair basketball team.

The first time Jeff attended a practice, he came home elated in a way he had not been for years. He loved the all-out way they played, smashing into each other, even knocking each other out of their wheelchairs. Practice soon became his favorite day of the week. It was great to get physical.

When the team entered a tournament in Redding, a four-hour drive away, Jeff's parents were concerned. Leland had offered to drive, but they didn't know him, and the trip would necessitate staying overnight in a motel.

"Right," Jeff said to their worries. "How many mass murderers do you know who are confined to a wheelchair?"

Seeing how much it meant to Jeff, they let him go.

Jeff found the tournament enjoyable, even though one of his teammates had a terrible seizure and had to be taken away by ambulance. The games wrapped up on Saturday night. On Sunday morning, Leland suggested to Jeff that they go to a church he knew. Jeff had no objection, so they wheeled their chairs into a sprawling structure known as Bethel Church. Jeff sat through the service and wasn't particularly struck by it.

After the service they invited people who wanted prayer to come forward. Leland wanted us both to go. I wouldn't have done it without his urging. I was not really hoping for anything, but I wheeled down to the front because Leland urged me. Two young people came up to us and prayed for us, laying hands on us. We weren't the center of attention. Other people were praying nearby.

I didn't feel anything while they prayed, and I really didn't think anything had happened. Then one of them said, "Jeff, stand up."

I did stand up. That was nothing special. I could always stand. I waited for the pain to start, as it always did. But this time it didn't. I took a few steps. No pain. Somebody suggested I should do something that would really hurt. I walked up on the stage, four feet high, and jumped to the ground. That should have been excruciating, but there was no pain. None. From that moment, I've never had another ounce of pain in my feet.

I was in shock. Most people had already left the church, but we hung around awhile, talking to people.

Jeff had spoken to me in a very matter-of-fact voice, but at this moment his eyes went into space. His words came out quietly, dreamily. "I'll always remember pushing my wheelchair down the aisle and out of that church."

Jeff didn't call his parents. They had no idea what had happened when he reached home that afternoon. "Mom,

Dad, guess what," he said, getting out of the car. "My feet aren't hurting." As she absorbed the news, his mom began to cry. Typical of Jeff, he didn't want to talk about it. He grabbed his skateboard. He hadn't used it in years, but he still remembered how.

Jeff's feet were like new, but his legs were the same old legs. He hadn't used them for years, and the muscles had atrophied. Skateboarding soon wore him out; walking was hard. His legs were so sore he had to use crutches for several days.

When he went to class on Monday, everybody wanted to know what had happened to him. All the years he had been in a wheelchair, nobody ever asked questions. Now he told the story over and over again. "The reactions were mixed. I could tell that some people just didn't believe me. Others were amazed. At church, reactions were also mixed. Many people were overjoyed. All my friends thought it was just awesome. But I could tell a lot of people didn't know what to think."

Jeff didn't begrudge anybody their doubts. "If it had been reversed, I would have been the same way."

2

Why a Miracle Matters, and How

I've spent lots of time around people who believe in miracles. I've participated in prayer meetings where we laid hands on people desperate for healing. I've attended many Pentecostal or charismatic services, hoping eagerly to see God work supernaturally. I've lived in Africa and traveled all over the world, hearing countless stories of miracles. But I had never been close enough to a miracle to be sure that one occurred.

I remember once, in a time of doubt, praying, "Lord, if you will just show yourself in some way that's unquestionable, I'll never doubt you again. Speak or act in a way that can only be you." I begged for some kind of proof of God's existence, but none came.

This wasn't an isolated occurrence—for most of my life I've wanted to witness something I could definitely, confidently claim was a miracle.

Now I have.

I believe what happened to Jeff Moore was a miracle, and when I see Jeff walking around, I'm reminded of it. The doctors had given up hope, but something changed in answer to prayer. The difference was instantaneous and unmistakable and enduring. After talking to Jeff, I knew it wasn't fake. I knew it wasn't hype or exaggerated emotion. It had to be God.

And yet, I didn't find myself jumping up and down. And I didn't find that all my doubts had vanished.

Why do I care about miracles? Why should anyone? I can offer two primary reasons.

The first has to do with faith. I believe in a God who made the universe out of nothing, who has extraordinary power and is alive and active today. That's the God of the Bible, who has claimed my life, and so I want to see his power at work. Many of my neighbors and friends deny that God's power exists at all. Miracles can blast through those doubts—theirs and mine—and make God's power manifest.

Then, at a much more existential level, I find that at times I am desperate. I have run out of resources to solve crucial problems and can offer nothing but my prayers. Sometimes the crisis comes as sickness, sometimes because of personal problems, sometimes because of natural disasters. When a friend is miscarrying, I ask God to save the baby's life. When a tornado is bearing down, I cry out for God to help in a direct and amazing way. Who doesn't? They say there are no atheists in foxholes.

This book is not addressed to the person who is convinced there are no miracles. Maybe real life will show you something to change your mind, but words on a page aren't likely to do so. (I'm well aware that my telling of Jeff's story is not enough to convince you.)

Neither is this book addressed to those who see miracles every time they turn around. If you have no questions about miracles, I don't particularly want to convince you that you should.

Though I start with Jeff's story, and though I will tell of other encounters with the miraculous, this book is not simply a collection of miracle stories. Rather, it is a guide to miracles—how to think about them, pray for them, respond to them (or respond to their absence). This book is a guide for how to live in God's world, and how to walk alongside him as he does his work. It's a book about faith and hope and love as they get worked out on planet earth.

I want to walk through some fundamental issues with you. For example, what *is* a miracle? Some say it's God doing the impossible, violating the laws of nature. Some say it's much broader than that. If we opened our eyes, they say, we would see miracles all the time—a rainbow, or a storm, or life itself.

We will sort through the questions of defining miracles. Very close to those issues are matters of science. Can a scientist believe in miracles? For lots of people, science obliterates the possibility of the miraculous. Is that really so?

I want to look closely at the Bible. Yes, many miracles occur there, but what kinds of miracles? Do miracles always happen when God is involved with people of faith? What did Jesus believe about miracles? What about Paul and the other apostles? What did they say miracles were for?

Beyond the Bible, it's helpful to consider the experiences of other Christians. I will survey the experiences of God's people through the centuries after Jesus. I'll examine the prevalence of miracles in other parts of the world today, particularly Africa, Asia, and Latin America. And I want to talk about the American church scene—especially the rise of charismatic and Pentecostal faith.

I'll also say a few words about what to do when God doesn't answer your prayers for miracles. How do you handle it if you're left out when miracles get distributed? People often talk about believing in a God of miracles. What about the God of non-miracles? How do you think and pray when God doesn't do what you long for?

In the end, I will sum up with practical advice, offering principles that have come out throughout the book. I hope these principles will help you live and walk with God in a way that pleases him.

"It's hard to believe what happened if you didn't go through the five years of pain with us." Sheri Moore, Jeff's mother, gave me a moving, blow-by-blow account of the agony they suffered, doctor after doctor, surgery after surgery.

"I felt that I was always fighting for my child. He was always very compliant, he never complained." But Sheri and her husband, Bob, were desperate to find some way to help.

"We talked Jeff into doing the last surgery," Sheri told me, with regret coloring her voice. By that time, Jeff had become resigned to his life in a wheelchair and didn't want to go under the knife ever again. Sheri always kept hoping.

When it became obvious that even the grueling refashioning of Jeff's foot had done no good, the Moores pushed hard for a consultation with a famous doctor at Stanford University Hospital. It was hard to convince their insurance company, but eventually they agreed to the expenditure. Sheri drove Jeff down.

"When we got to Stanford, it seemed like the land of hope. Everything was green and clean, polite and helpful. The atmosphere was night-and-day different from what we had become accustomed to." Surely a place like this would have the answer to Jeff's problems.

A student doctor did an initial evaluation and was very hopeful. "Then the real doctor came in. That was a shock. He was not happy. You could see that he was not happy at all.

" 'You need to stop,' he told us. 'No more surgeries. You have to get used to it. Jeff is going to be in a wheelchair. It's possible the pain will go away by itself, but we don't know what causes it, and we can't predict what will help it.'

"It knocked the wind out of me," Sheri remembers. "I got Jeff in the car, and then I broke down. I thought, *I can't do this anymore*. I had always been the cheerleader. I put Jeff's wheelchair in the back and I called Bob on the phone. I told him I couldn't get in the car. I was just crushed."

Eventually, she did get in the car and drove home. She had to try to accept it. They bought Jeff a $2,500 wheelchair and let him go on about his life. And they were utterly unprepared for what Jeff had to say when he came back from the basketball tournament.

Sheri actually knew about Bethel, the church where Jeff was healed. Its pastor has written books on healing; a friend had given Bob one, urging him to visit the church. Sheri and Bob seriously considered it, but in the end they decided not to go. All through his trials, Jeff's faith in God had remained intact. "We didn't want to mess with his faith. What if it doesn't work? At least he has God. And Jeff actually was never bitter about his feet. He was okay with his situation. He felt that there was some purpose to it. We were angry and upset, but I don't think he ever was."

Even after Jeff was healed, the Moores didn't visit Bethel. Leland, the friend who took Jeff there—and who was not healed himself—moved to Redding, feeling that he had to be part of what the church was doing. The Moores thought that same way at first. On reflection, though, they decided it was the wrong direction for them. "The place didn't heal my son," Sheri says. "God healed my son."

Nevertheless, she and Bob went through a time of questioning. "Who is our God? Are we acknowledging his full power?" They also struggled with judgmental feelings toward their home church—my church. Those who knew them well were overjoyed by their good news, but others showed less interest. "We wondered, *Are we at the wrong church?* We felt a little lost. It was really troubling. At first we thought everybody should want to process this with us."

For the Moores, Jeff's healing was the most wonderful thing that had ever happened to them—an impossible, joyful, astonishing reality. "Sometimes I see someone in a wheelchair and tears come to my eyes," Sheri says. "When Jeff was disabled, I thought that if only God would make him well, everything in our family would be absolutely perfect."

After his healing, Sheri feared the pain would come back. "I would watch Jeff on his skateboard and want to stop him, thinking, *You're going to mess it up!*"

But when other people expressed reservations or said, "I hope it holds," Sheri was put off. She didn't want to hear that.

Sheri didn't know it, but the story of Jeff's miraculous healing made a quiet impact on our church. Presbyterians aren't prone to jump and shout; they like to think about things. At least two couples made the four-hour trip to Bethel to be prayed for, including two very dear friends of mine, Tom and Joyce Bryant. Tom had Parkinson's disease and, as the disease progressed, he and Joyce decided that Bethel was an option they should explore.

Retired corporate executives, the Bryants were not the types to believe just anything. They spoke softly, dressed well, and appreciated their privacy. They told very few of their friends they were going to Bethel. I didn't know until much later.

After driving up on a Friday afternoon, they were struck by the friendliness and the youthfulness of an evening service. Even before worship began, two young women struck up a conversation and offered to pray for them. After the service, the Bryants went forward to ask for prayer. Prayer team members met them and prayed, assuring them, "God is going to heal you."

Saturday morning the Bryants went through a more involved process. First they filled out a detailed questionnaire, then they were called into a room where people trained in healing prayer talked to them and prayed for them. These healing ministers focused on Tom's difficult relationship with his father. Joyce listened to Tom talk about it and saw tears streaming down his face.

Tom was not healed of his Parkinson's. He recently died of it after a long and difficult struggle. But Joyce has nothing but good feelings about their experience at Bethel. Spiritual and emotional healing took place, she feels, and they were treated with love and respect. She and Tom had accepted that God chose not to heal Tom. They were thankful to Bethel for joining them in the request, even though it was not answered as they had hoped.

Another retired couple at my church, Bill and Florence Slyker, also traveled to Bethel. Both of them have a complicated history with healing miracles. Bill's first wife had been raised in a church that believed in miraculous healing, and when she became mentally ill, her mother asked Bill for permission to call the elders of her church to their home. The resulting loud and boisterous prayer service scared their children and did not result in healing. Bill's wife went to a mental hospital. The experience left a sour taste in Bill's mouth.

He later married Florence, who had also grown up in a church that emphasized healing, and the two of them attended meetings led by famous healers like Kathryn Kuhlman. Bill had an encounter with Kuhlman; her touch knocked him flat on his back. That countered his skepticism, but what really changed his mind was his own experience praying for Florence.

For years Florence had been plagued with severe headaches. She had pursued healing with a number of high-profile pastors, without success. One day an especially bad headache struck her, so she called Bill at work and asked him to come home. He was reluctant to do so. He was a man of meticulous routines, and he knew other family members were available to support Florence. As he pondered Florence's request, Bill told me, the Lord spoke to him: "What's the most important thing, your scheduled plans or your wife?"

He went home and found Florence in the bedroom. She asked him to pray for her, and he did. The headache vanished immediately and has not returned even once in the twenty years since.

Bill asked himself why the healing happened now, and not as she was prayed for by "all those great pastors." He concluded that the Lord had been waiting for him to pray for his wife. Telling his men's group about it, he began to cry, thinking that "maybe I could have prayed for her years ago and spared her all that pain."

When Bill was diagnosed with stomach cancer, his doctors told him that he probably had only a short time to live. Friends urged him to go to Bethel Church for healing, but he wasn't inclined to do so. "I didn't feel like I needed to go. I don't think we have to coax God for my healing. The whole church is praying for me. All my friends are praying. And whether I die of it or I am healed, I am a winner."

Eventually he went, but his experience wasn't as positive as the Bryants'. First the church mixed up his paper work, confusing his needs for healing with someone else's. Then they noticed he wore hearing aids.

"A girl spoke to me, and I said, 'You'll have to speak up because I don't hear very well.' She said, 'You have a hearing problem?' Right away they wanted me to take out my hearing aids so they could pray about my hearing."

When they finished praying for his ears the girl asked Bill if he could hear. "Yeah, sure," he said. He was never completely deaf, but "they began to announce to everybody, 'This man has been healed!' They brought a video camera over so I could tell the world. They made a big thing of it, while in reality nothing had occurred. I had to ask them to give me my hearing aids back."

When they prayed for his stomach cancer, they said they had a "laughing spirit," and bent over his stomach laughing at the cancer. "I know they were sincere," Bill says, "but it turned me off."

⌒⌒⌒

I'm convinced that, for Jeff Moore, a miracle took place at Bethel Church. I'm convinced partly because of the kind of person he is—no hype, no guile—but I'm also convinced by the astonishing turnaround. To go from crippling pain to no pain at all in the instant that praying hands were laid on him seems unexplainable in medical terms. (His surgeon takes the same view. When asked how he explains Jeff's condition, he simply says, "A miracle.")

This is a "sign and a wonder," to use biblical terminology. But the sign doesn't seem to communicate the same thing to everybody. If you think miracles prove God, you can't help but notice that not everybody responds to the proof. Jeff told anybody who was interested what had happened to him, but some didn't believe him. Even people in his own church had their doubts.

And notice what gets lost when the story spreads a step beyond the immediate experience. For Jeff's parents, the miracle was life-changing and beautiful beyond hope. For me, listening to Jeff tell his story in a coffee shop, it was compelling. For you, reading this account, it's likely to be less compelling. Maybe you retain doubts and questions. Some certainly do.

You can see testimonies of miracles on YouTube, and you can read about them in books and magazines. How many people really believe them? Probably only the people predisposed to believing them in the first place. Seeing is believing, but hearing secondhand is much less persuasive.

Sheri Moore told me that other churches invited her to tell about Jeff's healing, but she didn't take them up on it. "Talking to people one-on-one seems to be the way that makes sense," she says. She and Jeff even decided against talking at a Christmas service at our church. "I didn't want to grandstand it," Sheri says. "It was a holy event."

Their experience did make a difference for others, notably the two couples who traveled to Bethel Church. But each couple had their own experiences, which were nothing like Jeff's. One felt satisfied with love and spiritual encouragement. Another was turned off by the overeagerness in the people who prayed. None found physical healing.

Miracles are mysterious. There's no obvious reason why Jeff Moore was healed and Tom Bryant was not. There's no obvious reason why Jeff had to go to another city to have God take away his pain, when people—including his own parents—prayed for him at his own home church.

And there's no obvious reason why some people are moved to praise when they hear of Jeff's miraculous healing, while others are skeptical. Background beliefs surely play a part, but there is more to it than that.

All my life I've wanted God to show up in ways I can point to. I've never been totally satisfied with warm feelings and good morals alone; I want to see God at work in ways that can only be him.

From Jeff's experience, I learned that such things happen. They really do. They don't happen very often—if they did, we wouldn't call them miracles. But they do happen, and that gives me great encouragement.

However, I also learned that miracles don't have the broad and everlasting impact it seems they should. Some people are convinced—mostly people who were close to the people involved and can vouch for their credibility. Many more are not convinced. They shrug. They wonder. A few flatly state, "I don't believe it."

The farther out you go—to people who don't know the Moores but only hear of them secondhand, to television audiences and book readers—it seems the less impact you find.

What does God intend when he does a miracle? He's trying to get somebody's attention. He's communicating a message. What is the message? Who is it for? And why doesn't everybody believe?

3

Seeking Proof
of God

As I mentioned earlier, when I was in college I wanted God to show me he was real. As a committed believer, I didn't voice my doubts in public, but in the silence of my own mind, questions arose.

I now think those doubts had more to do with loneliness than philosophy. I had always been shy and introspective. I had friends—good friends—but sometimes I felt as desolate as a man lost on a high mountain. I longed for more. I ached for closeness at an age when I was most awkward about seeking it.

I put a lot of this loneliness on God. And why shouldn't I? The Bible tells of God's deep love for us, his promises not to abandon us. The Psalms speak in direct, personal terms to God, calling on him for comfort and help. I could identify with the psalmist. God *could* help me; why didn't he?

One particular night I remember walking through the neighborhoods near my college dorm, calling out to God. My request was quite simple: I wanted God to make himself unmistakably known to me. He could light up the sky with a message or he could whisper reassurance in my ear. I wasn't particular. I just wanted absolute assurance that he was real.

I kept walking and praying and waiting, but nothing happened. As the night progressed, I got more and more tired. Finally I ran out of steam. I gave up and went home to bed.

I slept, and in the morning my spiritual crisis didn't look quite so dramatic. I got out of bed, ate my breakfast, and went on with life.

I tell this very ordinary story on myself because it's typical of what draws many people to seek miracles. They want proof that God is real. And the reason they want proof is because they feel lonely and lost. They're convinced that if they knew God was absolutely real, they wouldn't feel so lost.

From the perspective of forty years later, I question that conviction. I'm no longer so sure that a miraculous intervention will make a stunning difference in how you feel.

I remember another wish that *has* been answered just as I imagined. I vividly remember thinking—and telling God—that if I could marry a wonderful woman, if I could only wake up each morning with a lovely female in my bed, I would be happy for the rest of my life. All complaints would stop.

I did marry such a woman, and I have been waking up in bed with her for thirty-three years. She is more lovely than I could have imagined at the age of twenty. But I am not always happy, and my complaining hasn't stopped. We deceive ourselves with the thought that if God just provided X—money, friends, success, love, miracles—all would be well forever. Our problems of loneliness and alienation do not lie in the realm of philosophy, and they are not solved by proof of God's existence. Our problems lie in ourselves.

Nevertheless, we seek proof. The proof may be in the form of healing miracles, or it may be more internal and invisible. Either way, we want an intervention that comes from outside ourselves—that is really God.

There's a Bible story in 1 Kings about the prophet Elijah. In chapter 18 he confronts the prophets of Baal on Mount Carmel. God sends down fire from heaven in answer to Elijah's prayers, Baal's prophets are routed, and everybody present falls to their knees shouting, "Yahweh!—He is God!" Miracles can't get more public.

But in chapter 19, Elijah's enemies resurge. He has to run for his life. At the end of a long and exhausting journey, deeply depressed, he ends up all alone in a cave. God speaks to him there, but not through the furious sounds of wind and earthquake. He speaks through a gentle whisper. His voice, which only Elijah hears, recharges Elijah and enables him to carry on his ministry with confidence.

Public miracles strengthen people and allay their doubts, but so can more interior revelations. What matters is the conviction that God is real and that he cares.

I met a man I'll call John Claassen. I had posted a request on my blog for anybody who had experienced miracles to write to me. John presented himself, telling me that he had a long, long story that embarrassed him terribly. He couldn't bear to talk about it publicly, but he was desperate for someone to help him understand what it meant.

In long interactions with John, I found him a deeply sincere, thoughtful, and searching man. He was humble, admitting that he didn't understand a lot of what had happened to him.

I mention this because John's story is well outside my comfort zone, and it may be outside of yours. It features a worldview permeated with supernatural happenings, both physical and spiritual. Here miracles are not once-in-a-lifetime events interrupting a regular flow of life. All of life is permeated with God's interventions and God's messages.

To some, John's story will seem quite bizarre. In many radical charismatic and Pentecostal churches, though, it will sound familiar. Such movements, which are increasingly prominent in our world, challenge us to rethink what is normal.

John's experiences go beyond what we usually think of as miracles, because most of them aren't physical. Is a word from God a miracle? A prophetic dream? We don't usually describe them that way. (I'll deal with the definition of *miracle* in the next chapter.) For now, though, think in terms of God breaking into our world in ways that astound us. That's the kind of miracle John was looking for, and that's what he found.

He was raised, John told me, in a very conservative Christian environment that didn't believe in miracles. But he had an inquiring mind. From his teenage years, he was determined to find the truth and live by it, and that's how he joined the charismatic movement.

It began with the Bible. How could he take its message seriously, he wondered, if none of the supernatural powers he read about were available anymore? Seeking to know for himself whether miracles still occurred, John got involved at a charismatic church camp. The preaching there emphasized that if you had enough faith, you would see miraculous healings, and if you didn't, then you needed to get more faith.

"I spent a lot of time trying to get more faith." He wanted to speak in tongues, and the camp leaders instructed him and others to start making random noises, letting "God inhabit the babble." He did what the leaders suggested, but he went home feeling dirty. "It was far too phony for me to buy in to."

John was searching, almost desperately, for something that would demonstrate God's reality breaking into everyday events. The last straw came when the camp's leading preacher gave a sermon urging them to take more risks in asking God to heal. He said that their fears held them back and kept them from seeing healing miracles. The talk made a huge impression on John.

After the service, John and some of his friends were playing basketball. There was a collision, and one of them lost a front tooth. "Full of faith, we marched straight to the preacher. After a sermon like that, we figured this would be a cinch." But the preacher disappointed them. He wouldn't even pray over the tooth. Saying that God uses doctors, he sent them off to one. "So much for charismatic healing bravado, which apparently comes only when you have an audience and a microphone in your hand."

Disillusioned, John dropped out. It could have been the end of his faith, he says, but a small flame of hope endured. Maybe there were other Christians who weren't manufacturing faith—Christians who experienced miracles that were more than hype.

Then John read a book about the Vineyard movement. "Within the charismatic movement, there is so much emphasis on having faith, and if nothing happens, it's your fault," John says. The Vineyard's message was different: it preached that miracles are in God's hands, not ours.

John found a Vineyard church in his city. "This is when things started getting weird, in the good way I had been hoping for."

In one of the first meetings John attended, his pinky finger started whipping back and forth, as though it had a life of its own. John watched it, fascinated. He knew that it wouldn't impress anybody else who saw it or heard about it. Who cared that his finger twitched? But for him it was gigantic. He wasn't doing it. He didn't think he could do it if he tried. Something outside himself was making his finger twitch.

A three-month "baptism period" followed in which uncanny experiences occurred nearly every day. They seemed to come out of nowhere, unexpected and unexplained. Once, John walked through a doorway and found himself knocked over backward and stuck flat on the floor for ten minutes. "I have no idea what that was about," John says.

Another time, during a prayer meeting, he started spinning like a figure skater, one foot on the floor and the other pedaling like a bicyclist to keep himself going around. It was a physical feat he has never been able to duplicate since, but at the time it was perfectly effortless. He watched himself do it as though he were an outside observer.

> I remember thinking to myself, "Wow, I'm experiencing a real miracle. I totally can't deny the supernatural nature of this one."
>
> Such is my personality. Even if something miraculous seems to be happening, I'm still asking questions to ensure that it's real. That approach is considered un-faith in the movements I was in, and it eventually gets you pushed to the edges. I still won't apologize for it. I think God is up to the challenge. In fact, it is exactly because I've experienced stuff that I found to be real that I don't want to settle for hype or embellishment. My very skeptical and analytic mind wouldn't put up with faking stuff. What happened to me was undeniable.

I say undeniable, but as I look back, the things that happened are quite deniable by anyone watching. People observing the behaviors I exhibited could have said (and very likely did say) that I was an overdramatic faker. Before it happened to me, that is precisely what I thought. The undeniable part, though, was what was going on inside me. I knew I wasn't faking. The stuff that was happening was unbelievably weird, but I wasn't doing it. That's still really hard for me to explain. The elders would tell us that you are always in control. God doesn't overwhelm your control. I still wonder about that, because I definitely felt at times like that was not the case.

Physical feats impressed John, but the prophetic words that came to him almost daily were more significant.

It started off when, in prayer, I suddenly started singing in a Hebrew-sounding language. It was such a beautiful song that even now tears come to my eyes as I recall it. The weird thing is how detached from the moment I felt. I seemed to be the regular old me, sitting there in my body, as someone or something used my mouth and voice to sing. I described it at the time as feeling "possessed" by the personality of an old, passionate Jewish guy. "Possessed," I was told, was definitely not the way to think of it or describe it. "Possessed" was a word to be avoided. I did what I was told, but if I am speaking honestly, that's sure what it felt like. After the song, I jumped up and proceeded to preach and gesture and act things out for probably over an hour. Two friends were with me the whole time. Whatever I was doing seemed intended to communicate a message, but we couldn't really make out what it could be.

That scene initiated the next three months of weirdness. I would constantly shake and roar, making every noise and blip you can imagine. When I walked into a room, it was as though a tractor beam pointed me toward one or two people. I could feel a word was coming, so I patiently waited. Then I would start shaking, and nonsense gibberish would come from my mouth, eventually transforming into English. I would yell things in English to the people I was focused on. It might take an hour altogether. In the Vineyard that didn't seem long—we had time to wait on the Lord.

What made it feel so miraculous was that I didn't seem to have any control over my words, or even know what words were coming. That led to my giving some extremely bold words. Afterward I would feel scared that I had said such things.

For three months John had such experiences almost every day. The rest of the time he lived like a normal person. He was a music leader in worship, and he led a small group Bible study. The church regarded him a sterling example of what God can do in someone's life.

"To this day I don't know whether I prophesied anything that was verifiably true. That seems to be a problem with prophecy: it's usually so subjective that it can't be analyzed in a scientific way. It wasn't the sort of thing that would bring a skeptic to faith."

But it did bring John to deeper faith, because the presence of God in his life was so undeniably real. After three months, his prophetic gift faded out. He became more cautious about speaking, nervous that he would express his own ideas rather than God's. Sometimes, out of caution, he said nothing. He is still not sure if that was a mistake.

Over the next four years, life settled down. John got married, became a schoolteacher, and took a job in Japan. He stayed involved with his Vineyard church, but God's involvement in his life was more ordinary.

When he came back to Canada after several years abroad, he started a band with a drummer friend, Robbie. Music had always been "the road not taken" for John. Now he and Robbie felt they were making very good music, and they wished they could take the next step and record a CD.

It takes money to record, but they didn't have any. One day, sitting in John's basement, they began to lament how broke they were. They didn't often talk this way, which made the out-of-the-blue phone call seem all the more remarkable.

The caller was the wife of a well-known local music producer, calling on her cell phone from a restaurant. She said, "I know that this will sound really weird, but I'm sitting here with Andrew. He's shaking and manifesting the Holy Spirit, and he says I am supposed to tell you that God says if you guys want to make a CD, he'll do it for nothing."

This, John says, was a $15,000 phone call. He and Robbie were overwhelmed with excitement. Not only would they get to make a recording, but the supernatural nature of the message convinced them that God had something huge in mind.

The more they thought about it, the more excited they became. God wanted to use their music. They were going to be the next U2.

Then the dreams began. John's pregnant wife dreamed that their baby was born six months early, and it grew faster and bigger than anyone could have expected.

Soon after that, a woman in their church, without any knowledge of that dream, prophesied that something major would happen in July. Then dream after dream about the

baby came to various people—a meteor shower of prophecies suggesting that a baby would be born in July, a baby
that would show uncommon growth. John began to see the
dreams as symbolic because, in reality, the baby was due in
January, not July. But July was the month they planned to go
into the recording studio.

When July came, they made the CD with sky-high expectations, and by November they were shopping the demo to
music distributors. John's excitement reached a fever pitch.
Any day, any hour, a phone call would come. But it took longer than he had expected. He began to fast and pray, asking
God for direction.

During his years in Japan, John had periodically asked
God to direct him to a verse in the Bible that would give him
guidance. He would open the Bible at random and put his
finger down on the page. Whatever verse he found, he would
take as a message from God. Twice he had been directed to
a verse in 2 Chronicles: "Hezekiah was twenty-five years old
when he became king, and he reigned in Jerusalem twenty-
nine years" (29:1). The verse never made any sense to John.

Now, fasting and praying for direction about the CD, John
"got" a verse he had never seen before: 2 Kings 18:3. He was
amazed to find that it came immediately after a verse that
repeated the exact same passage he had found in 2 Chronicles.
Verse 3 reads, "He did what was right in the eyes of the Lord,
just as his father David had done." But verse 2 was word-for-
word the same as 2 Chronicles 29:1. In the Vineyard, John had
been taught that human beings are imperfect vessels for the
Holy Spirit; sometimes the message needs a commonsense
adjustment. John assumed that due to human error, he was
one verse off; the correct verse must be verse 2.

He didn't know the Bible all that well. Until that moment, he had no idea that 2 Kings and 2 Chronicles repeat each other. Clearly, he thought, this was a supernatural event. Now the message that had seemed obscure years before made perfect sense. He, John, was twenty-five years old. He was going to be made "king."

At this point, I suspect some readers may be in supernatural overload. John is beginning to seem a bit crazy. But the very ethos of the Vineyard movement, and many movements like it, is a universe permeated with God's continual, active presence. Prophetic dreams, astonishing coincidences, supernatural messages, and divine directives are normal, not exceptional. And who can say they're not? Isn't that the ethos of the Bible?

John's baby was born January 1, 2001, just after the stroke of midnight. As had been prophesied, he wasn't any ordinary baby. He was the New Millennium baby for the whole city. TV crews and newspaper journalists appeared at the hospital, and John's family's faces were displayed all over the news. This seemed to underline the dramatic and supernatural way that God had taken control of their lives. If the "natural" baby was a celebrity, surely the "supernatural" baby born in July would be even more so.

But still the phone call did not come. The CD got encouraging responses from some people, but there were no signs that it would take off. John's birthday is March 16. He would be twenty-six. Since the biblical passage spoke of becoming king at the age of twenty-five, John "knew" that the breakthrough had to come by 11:59 p.m. on March 15.

He stayed up all night, waiting. Nobody called. Nothing happened.

From that day on, hope began to wither away. The CD never made a splash. John and his wife found themselves badly in debt, largely from costs incurred when the band went on a promotional tour. John and his wife became depressed and despairing. Eventually they decided he would have to give up on music and they'd go back to Japan. They have been in Japan for several years now, teaching school and raising their children. Disappointment has faded, but John still doesn't know what to make of his experience.

> Looking back I can see how our desire for "bigness" is not at all the heart of God. In the charismatic world, prophecies and their interpretations are usually about things becoming HUGE.
>
> So was God playing a great big trick to humble us? That would seem kind of mean.
>
> I would like to be able to say that we just made it all up, a bunch of over-hyped young dreamers who read too much into stuff. But the concrete events—my son's perfectly timed arrival, the amazing phone call—make it hard for me to do that.
>
> I will say there's no way I'd be a believer today were it not for the undeniable weird things that happened to me in my early twenties. I believe strongly that there are things going on in that "God" realm. But I highly distrust those who think they have the hows and whys all figured out. I know that they don't.

John has carried on in faith even if his questioning mind sometimes makes him doubt. When he talks about his miraculous experiences today, he mostly asks questions. "I can't deny that something happened, but what was it for?" Though he's far less bitter than he was, there's still an edge of resentment in John's thoughts. He wants to say to God, "If you're not going to talk sense, please don't talk at all."

My long and probing conversation with John reminded me of other conversations I have had over the years. When you go deep with people, they sometimes tell you of times in their lives when God seemed to enter with blazing clarity. But that clarity doesn't necessarily continue.

For example, a good friend told me of a summer she spent abroad during college, when in desperate loneliness and angst she couldn't sleep and became exhausted to the point of desperation. At her darkest moment, crying out to God in prayer, she found herself praying in a language she didn't understand. For hours she went on praying fluently in this mysterious language, feeling the closest linkage to God. She could pray freely and fully. It saved her. After that she was calm and could sleep, and she completed her summer in good shape.

She has been through terribly hard times in her life since, much harder times, in fact, but that prayer language never returned.

Why was God so clearly present at one time, while now he appears more distant and mysterious? What does it mean? Life with God can be mystifying, and sometimes we get disappointed. Most people don't talk about such experiences. It's easier to keep them to ourselves.

When I encountered John, I was studying Genesis with a small group from my church. We had just finished reading the chapters in which Abraham's life comes to an end. As I pondered John's story, I also pondered Abraham.

Like John, Abraham had amazing and uncanny encounters with the living God. God spoke to him, announcing his presence and telling of an astonishing future. God said he was taking a special interest in Abraham's life. Abraham would be especially blessed, and the blessings he experienced were not just for him and his family, but for the entire world.

Abraham heard promises from God larger than anything John could have imagined—much bigger than a hot CD.

At the end of his life, though, Abraham had very little to show for it. The man to whom God had promised a vast expanse of the Middle East possessed only a tiny sliver of land, a cave where his wife was buried and he would be, too. And the man whom God had promised descendants as numerous as the stars in the sky had a single son born of that covenant, Isaac. As to the promise that God would use Abraham to bless the whole world—Abraham had no down payment on that at all. He was a nomadic sheepherder living in a tent, nothing more.

Abraham had one strong conviction, which he shared with his servant while sending him off to find a wife for Isaac: "Make sure that you do not take my son back [to Mesopotamia]" (Genesis 24:6). Abraham had followed God from Mesopotamia to the Promised Land. He was determined never to go back, nor for his descendants to go back.

Abraham was committed to staying on God's path, even though much of the rest of his life must have confused him. What could he make of those uncanny encounters with God, like the time when he was told to kill animals and cut them in half, setting them out under the stars until a torch and a smoking firepot passed between them? (See Genesis 15.)

What about the time he was instructed to make a blood sacrifice of his son, and then at the last moment he was told not to? (See Genesis 22.) Or the time when he was told to circumcise not just himself but his whole extended family, including servants? (See Genesis 17.) What did these things mean? Abraham didn't know. God's purposes were far from clear. Abraham's life only began to make sense two thousand years later, through his offspring, Jesus.

In Jesus it made some sense that Abraham had been told to sacrifice his son and then was told not to. God demanded such an ultimate gift as proof of Abraham's faith, but in Jesus he provided a substitute. Jesus completed the story of Abraham's sacrifice: God gave his own Son so that Abraham didn't have to. (And neither do we.)

The chosen people numbered like the stars in the sky? The promised blessing to the whole world? That began to happen when Jesus opened the blessings of the chosen people to the universe, adopting all comers into his family. Not only Palestine, but the whole world belonged to Abraham's heirs. Abraham became the father of a multitude, and a blessing to the ends of the earth. In Christ, his life and God's promises begin to add up.

I don't pretend to comprehend what happened in John's year of prophetic excitement, but I will say this: Christian experiences, like Abraham's, can only be fully interpreted in the light of Christ. His life, death, and resurrection, his rule over the whole earth, are the thread on which everything must hang.

Maybe John misinterpreted the prophecies. Maybe the baby being born was not a musical CD; maybe the child being born was John. And maybe John really did become "king" that year. His faith, after all, grew strong, even though his CD did not.

Jesus does not care much about successful CDs; he cares about human lives. John is one of those people Jesus cares about. And John's life is still growing, pushing up from the soil of those mysterious experiences with God.

Do I understand what happened to John? No, not really. But I know that God has him in his grip and will never let go. And I think those weird experiences, at the very least, grabbed John and held him close.

I've told about John at some length because it introduces us further into the mystery of miracles. God really does amazing things, but

- not always in ways that make sense to us;
- not always in ways that we want;
- not always in completely holy and admirable circumstances.

Regarding that last point, sometimes I meet people who attend miracle-believing churches but end up deeply disappointed by something the pastor or the elders did. Maybe the pastor demanded total authority over their lives. Maybe he or she manipulated the congregation. Maybe the pastor and elders enriched themselves at others' expense. Such things happen.

Miracle-believing churches are very human structures with very human problems—like all other churches. We look for miracles, and if we find them, they are situated in the squalor of ordinary life, surrounded by the faults of human beings. So it was in the Bible. So it is today.

Think about Abraham. He had undeniable encounters with the living God. Things happened that he could not explain apart from God, but such privileges didn't make Abraham's life neat and tidy. Many of his experiences were more confusing than illuminating. Nor was he a perfectly admirable character. He lied. His family life was a mess.

When you probe deeply into people's encounters with God, you often find this pattern. God is there, but so is everything else. It's not all pretty, and it's often confusing. It will only make perfect sense in the light of the face of God, revealed in Jesus Christ when we see him finally and fully. Come, Lord Jesus.

4

Why Don't People Believe?

John Claassen sought miracles because he had doubts. He wanted reassurance that God is real and active today, not just in history.

Miraculous events answered John's doubts. Yes, he remained very unsure of what God was telling him through those miracles, but the miracles convinced him there is a God. He is real. He does amazing things.

Miracles are clear evidence of God's power working in the world. Why, then, don't more people believe? Why do so many doubters and skeptics remain?

In this chapter I want to take up some of the reasons doubters give. I also want to answer the question, "Just what *are* miracles?" Many doubts about miracles begin with confused thinking and vague definitions.

Let me begin with the more superficial reasons people disbelieve in miracles. John Claassen's first camp experiences, with the hype and hypocrisy he perceived, offer a good example of one reason people disbelieve. Some people who attend healing services are turned off by what they feel is fakery. Others find that when they look in to reports of miracles, the stories are exaggerated or can't be verified.

People exaggerate. People pass on stories without checking their facts. People eagerly report miracles where there aren't any. (Remember my friend Bill and his hearing aids?)

Some Christian circles inadvertently encourage exaggeration. They create an atmosphere where Christians feel obliged to believe reports of miracles. If you express skepticism or suggest that more information is needed, they show disappointment in your lack of faith. True Christians, it seems, don't have doubts; they experience miracles everywhere they turn.

I'll say it loud and clear: I believe in miracles, but I don't believe in most reports of miracles. As a journalist, I've found that the evidence for miracles is sometimes very hard to locate. I recall interviewing John Wimber, a founder of the Vineyard movement who had published several books describing the amazing miracles of healing and prophecy done in his church. When you read Wimber's books, you can't help but believe that amazing miracles happened all the time.

When I asked whether I could interview some of those people, though, neither Wimber nor his staff could help me locate them. Some had moved away with no forwarding address. None seemed to be active members of the church.

I'm not suggesting the reports were phony. I believe Wimber was an honorable man whom God used. But I strongly suspect that stories of healing miracles got passed along without much scrutiny—and that the picture he painted of rampant miracles was exaggerated.

Exaggerated reports or credulous responses have a way of undermining genuine witness. Loads of people are convinced that miracles never happen, because they just don't believe the stuff they see on TV. And they may be right not to.

Having given credit to the skeptics, however, let me say something on the other side. Skepticism about *most* reports should never blind us to the possibility that *some* reports really are true. Historians have said that if all the basements in Ohio that are said to have harbored escaping slaves before the Civil War had *genuinely* harbored escaping slaves, there would have been no slaves left in the South. So should you conclude that the Underground Railroad was a myth? No. Some slaves escaped, and some Ohioans hid them in their basements. Among all the exaggerated and false claims, some are true. And if some are true, that's significant.

It's the same with miracles. If you look into it, you'll find miraculous reports that become murky—or disappear altogether—when you get close. Other reports, though, are deeply credible and would shake the faith of any honest unbeliever. The Catholic church, most notably, has a cautious and systematic process for certifying miracles—and they *do* certify some. To certify someone as a saint, for example—as was done with Mother Teresa—an investigation must show that the saint's prayers led to miraculous signs. Healings have to be demonstrated conclusively to a panel of doctors and scholars. The person prayed for must have been sick with an incurable disease and have been cured spontaneously, instantaneously, completely, lastingly, and in a way that doctors cannot explain by natural processes.

New Testament scholar Craig Keener, author of *Miracles: The Credibility of the New Testament Accounts,* reports on hundreds if not thousands of miracles that he learned of from trustworthy sources. But he told me that authentication was surprisingly hard to get. Most people don't keep medical records from before their sickness, during their sickness, and after their sickness. That kind of proof is hard to obtain. Nevertheless, some miracles do meet the strictest standards of authentication.

People also disbelieve because they haven't seen the miracle for themselves. They'll ask, "Have you ever seen water turned into wine? Ever seen somebody walk on water?"

Okay, I haven't seen such things firsthand, but what does that prove? I believe in lots of things I haven't personally witnessed. Almost everything that I read in the news is beyond my personal experience. I wasn't there for WWII, but I am sure it occurred. I didn't see the Twin Towers fall, but I have no doubt it happened. I've never walked on the moon, but I believe the witness of those who did.

It gets more personal than that. I can't remember the day of my birth, but I believe my parents when they say it was an icy day in Monessen, Pennsylvania. A friend of mine says she paddled a canoe across most of Canada. I wasn't there, but I believe her.

I'm convinced that Jeff Moore's case is genuine. So is John Claassen's. And so are many others. I believe in them because I believe the people who tell me about them. There is strong and trustworthy testimony that something amazing occurred, something that points toward a living and active God.

Miracles can't be scientifically tested, for the simple reason that they are, by definition, historical events. They can't be replicated in an experiment any more than you can replicate Napoleon's decisions at the Battle of Waterloo. If you want to test the truth of a miracle, or the truth of what happened at Waterloo, you have to use the methods of historians or court-room lawyers. You have to summon testimony and evidence.

Testimony and evidence hardly ever make a slam-dunk case. People's memories are faulty, and eyewitness testimony is notoriously unreliable. Still, with care, you can reach conclusions. The courts do it all the time. So do the history books.

I know people who, if they look me in the eye and say something happened, I believe it happened. They are sober, careful, utterly truthful, and modest. I trust their character and their reliability.

GOD AND THE MECHANICAL WORLD

In the case of miracles, even reliable testimony won't penetrate some people's doubts. Why? Because they have background beliefs that keep them from believing that testimony.

In the late seventeenth century, a very devout Christian, Isaac Newton, applied his amazing mind to unraveling the secrets of the universe. Many people think Newton was the most brilliant and influential man in history. His thought ranged far in many directions—he wrote more about theology than physics—but he is best remembered for his contributions to science and mathematics. His discovery of gravity and the laws of motion enabled him to analyze the planetary orbits of the solar system. He invented calculus in order to make precise calculations, enabling astronomers to track each planet and moon so precisely you could set your watch by the moons of Jupiter. Everything was perfectly in its place and completely predictable. An image of a silent, perfect, mechanical universe grew up—the universe as a machine.

We have grown up with this image and find it hard to grasp how revolutionary it was. Before Newton, the natural world seemed so uncannily alive that many people worshiped it. And why not? Watch the night sky and you see something mysterious and awe-inspiring—quite deserving of worship, actually, compared with most of what people settle for.

Newton and other pioneers of physics and astronomy probed so deeply into the processes of nature that all the mysteries of the night sky seemed to dissipate. The planets were reduced to vast accumulations of rock and gas circling helplessly around the sun. What once threw people into hysteria—the blotting out of the sun in a solar eclipse—now became merely an interesting and predictable mechanical phenomenon.

Then other sciences began to make their contributions—biology, particularly, with its discovery of genetics. Not only the solar system, but also a tree could be fully explained through "laws of nature" that described the way its mechanism worked—and has to work. So could animals, including humans. Diseases, once the province of evil spirits or bad humors, could be explained by the predictable workings of minute organisms. And diseases could be cured! Put all this knowledge together and you get the world as a complex and well-oiled machine, running on its own, without God needing to do anything.

Naturally, many people who come to believe in such a mechanical universe eventually become skeptics about God. "I had no need for that hypothesis," one French astronomer, Pierre-Simon Laplace, was reported to tell Napoleon when asked about the place of the Creator in his work.

Others become deists who believe God wound up the world like a clock and let it run. They still believe in God, but not that he gets involved with the physical world. Their God is a Spirit who offers inspiration for moral and spiritual living.

Still, some people maintain belief in an active God. They recognize the machine-like aspect of creation, but they insist that God is still alive. If so, how does he show it? They say he occasionally intervenes in the world in a supernatural way. They divide the world into "nature" and "supernature"—between the way the world runs on its own, like a machine, and the occasional interventions of God. Newton, for example, thought that God occasionally had to step in to adjust the planets in their orbits, lest they get out of synchrony.

Supernatural events, by this way of thinking, are occasions when God interferes with the natural machinery and does something different. He steps in and zaps the cancer. He turns the water into wine. He puts his finger on a gear in the machine of nature and makes it turn in a different direction.

People who absolutely separate nature from supernature call these supernatural occasions when God steps in "miracles."

This way of thinking has led to a crisis for believers. The more we learn about the universe, the smaller the spaces for these miracles. Science goes deeper and deeper in its understanding, and the God of miracles is hardly left a crack to operate in.

For example, a century ago, people would die of diseases without warning and without explanation. If a child came down with a deathly fever, people would pray desperately. And if the child recovered, you could call that a miracle of God. He had stuck his finger in and stopped the disease.

Nowadays, we use lab tests to understand the nature of the illness, we apply healing drugs, we put in an IV to combat dehydration—and when the child gets well, we thank the doctors. Did God's involvement get smaller? If medicine achieved absolute mastery, healing every disease, would God disappear?

In order to make space for God, Christians who believe in the natural/supernatural division keep arguing against science—that it really doesn't know so much. But that's a losing argument in this scientific era. No wonder lots of people regard miracles as something that disappeared with the Middle Ages. For them, those testifying to a miracle might as well be testifying to a fire-breathing dragon.

This, I think, is the main reason reports of miracles don't penetrate people's minds. In their mental framework, there's no space for miracles. Science has so thoroughly filled out our knowledge of events, there's no room left for supernature.

Unless a miracle hits them in the eye, they aren't convinced when someone tells them about one. The reports don't fit their mental image of the universe.

But go a little deeper, and you'll realize this division between natural and supernatural is both unbiblical and unscientific.

Scripture teaches that God never lets go of his handiwork; he is intimately involved in everything that happens in the physical universe. Perhaps the book of Colossians states this most comprehensively when it says Jesus is "the firstborn over all creation. . . . In him all things were created. . . . In him all things hold together. . . . For God was pleased to have all his fullness dwell in him, and through him to reconcile to himself all things, whether things on earth or things in heaven. . . ." (Colossians 1:15–20).

From the beginning to the end, Jesus Christ has his hands on "all things." Everything holds together in him and will have its reconciliation in him. It is quite incorrect to think of the world whirling along on its own, with God occasionally dipping in to adjust things.

Much of the problem arises, as G. K. Chesterton wrote, from people misinterpreting the regularity of nature. They take repetition to be the sign of machinery, impersonally repeating itself. But there is another kind of repetition that is not mechanical at all. A child can hear the same story every night for a year, can enjoy the same trick or the same cuddle endlessly. If you swing a child in the air, he says, "Do it again!" long past the time you are sick of it. Children don't get tired of repetition, and neither, Chesterton says, does God. He delights in it. Every time the sun rises he shouts out, "Do it again!"

The implication is that trees and the sun and babies are not merely signs of what God did sometime in the past. They are not windup toys that he set in motion long ago. Everything they do in their regular and predictable way, they do through his presence and his power.

Wherever we look in the natural world, we see God at work. What we call the natural laws are really just reports on his usual way of operating. He activates and supervises the natural laws; he shouts with delight at their working.

Some skeptics think that if they can describe the physical process behind an event, then they have eliminated God from it. They don't realize that God is exuberantly involved in the physical process.

Does that mean that everything is a miracle? If everything that happens is a work of God, can we call every baby's birth and every blooming rose a miracle? Is a tree a continuing miracle?

There's a simple answer to that: no. Because if everything that happens is a miracle, why call it a miracle? Why not just call it an event?

I sympathize with the sentiment behind calling everything a miracle. Each sunrise and every baby's birth is astonishing and beautiful, a sign of God, and if they happened once in a generation, we would drop everything and stare at them in sheer amazement. If no one had ever seen a sunrise, and then one morning you did, it would strike you speechless. As is, sunrises, while very beautiful, are so common that very few of us even get out of bed to witness them. If a friend woke you tomorrow morning to tell you the sun was rising, you might be annoyed.

That's why *miracle* is a poor word choice for a sunrise or a baby's birth or a tree turning color. We save this word for those events that are so unusual, so unexpected, that we can't help being astonished. "Signs and wonders" is the term Scripture often uses. True miracles cause us to wonder, and they point, like signs, to something extraordinary beyond themselves.

Put it that way, and you see there is no sharp boundary between the miraculous and the non-miraculous. They are simply different ways of describing God's activity. God has his hands on both. Both can give us reasons to praise him. There is no conflict between the "natural" and the "supernatural." Everything is natural and supernatural at the same time.

In fact, the non-miracles that God does every day should astonish us. The nuclear fusion of the sun? The ponderous and unstoppable movement of the earth's crust? The electrical flashes of a human brain? Those happen constantly, but they are nevertheless amazing. The ordinary is really extraordinary.

The ordinary is full of God's supernatural glory. Science describes and measures these, but it never really explains them. Gravity is a marvel beyond explaining. We can quantify its power, but we never understand why.

Miracles, though, are a distinct kind of marvel. You could argue that Jesus' feeding the five thousand was an insignificant event compared to the annual wheat crop. Think about how astonishing and wonderful wheat is. Can you grasp the process by which one small, dull, dead-looking, dried-up seed can turn out green shoots and make itself into a plant? And how that plant grows tall and reproduces the original seed a hundred times? That is a marvel far more significant than Jesus' expanding one boy's lunch into food for five thousand. After all, the wheat crop feeds billions, and does it again and again.

Yet nobody is surprised by wheat. We take the wheat crop for granted because it happens every year in thousands of locations. It is God's regular work, whereas Jesus' use of a boy's lunch to feed a large crowd was something nobody had ever seen. It astonished the crowd, and it pointed toward the truth that Jesus is the nourisher and provider, even in the most improbable circumstances. It was a miracle not because it was more superb or more important than the wheat crop, but because it was utterly unusual and unexpected, and because it was the vehicle God used to convey an important message about Jesus.

When we understand that God is everywhere and that everything happens supernaturally, it changes how we think. Suppose my child is sick and I am deeply worried. How do I pray for her?

"God, please show up!" is a very natural way to feel, but it is not a good way to pray. In fact, God is not absent; he is intimately present. He has never stopped working with my child. His Spirit holds her together, gives her breath, energizes the healing potential of her body. Knowing he is there, working, I pray humbly, asking him to heal her.

Am I asking him to do something different from what he is already doing? Perhaps not. Perhaps healing is already at work, only I cannot see it. I do not understand my daughter's illness, and I am not in a position to counsel God on how to uphold her life. But I can talk to him. I can tell him what I long to see. He wants me to ask and tells me I should. But I must ask humbly, knowing that he cares much more for my child than I can ever imagine. I am not requesting that he break his own rules; I ask that he carry on his rules of healing with my child. I am not asking him to get involved; I am thanking him for his involvement and for opening my heart to him about what I long to see through his care.

And when my daughter gets well, I thank God for healing her. Was it a miracle? That depends. Was she near death? Were the doctors perplexed and unable to offer much hope? Then her healing may be called a miracle, because it was a wonder. But whether or not we call it a miracle, we have certainly seen the hand of God in healing.

Sometimes it is very hard to say whether an event should be called a miracle. What makes a miracle for one person may be something else for another, because we all bring different expectations and different senses of what is "normal." Truthfully, the question of what we call a miracle isn't terribly important. What matters is that we see God's involvement and thank him.

SCIENCE AND THE LAWS OF NATURE

What about events that aren't just surprising, but seem impossible? What about walking on water, turning water into wine, rising from the dead? These are unlike healing miracles, where natural processes that we see operating every day may be involved.

Doesn't science deny that such miracles are possible because they violate the laws of nature? Are they not impossible by definition? And shouldn't a logical mind conclude that the impossible is impossible?

This was the famous objection of the philosopher David Hume, who wrote, "A miracle is a violation of the laws of nature; and as a firm and unalterable experience has established these laws, the proof against a miracle, from the very nature of the fact, is as entire as any argument from experience can possibly be imagined."

When you add up the sum of human experience, Hume says, you get natural laws. Apples fall down, not up. The sun rises in the east and sets in the west. Human experience has found it to be invariably so, and we sum up these experiences as "laws of nature." Miracles go against that. Hume is saying that we have to judge truth by experience, summed up in the natural laws. That's the scientific point of view.

The deceptive part of Hume's argument is calling scientific observations "the law of nature." The word "law" makes it sound like it is illegal to do anything else. But the law of nature is just a way of saying that this is how it always happens, every time we notice. This is the sum of human experience. If it were to happen some other way, it would not violate any law. It would simply be an unexpected and unprecedented occurrence, which is exactly what a miracle claims to be.

Hume says miracles never happen? Well, plenty of people testify that they do. To see who is right, we have to judge carefully to determine what testimony is reliable—not use the circular argument that miracles don't happen because human experience says they don't. Hume's argument is at its weakest here, though generations have taken it a great deal more seriously than it deserves to be taken.

Where Hume is a great deal more convincing, however, is in his questioning the reliability of witnesses.

Hume notes that people love to pass on amazing stories, and even embellish them. People are superstitious and eager to believe in the unbelievable. Human testimony is therefore not all that reliable. So if someone claims to have seen a miracle, their testimony has to be weighed against the experience of humankind, summed up in those "natural laws." It's prudent to be very skeptical when someone claims to have seen something that, according to all experience, doesn't happen.

As a journalist, I've learned to be skeptical when people tell me things. If somebody says that ten thousand people came to a meeting, I suspend judgment until I get a similar count from a variety of good sources. After all, people like to exaggerate crowds. All the more, then, if somebody tells me that they saw the whole crowd lift off the ground and hang in space for ten seconds. It would require much testimony from many reliable witnesses for me to take that claim seriously.

But that is not the same as saying that it can't happen.

If God has his hands on everything, then who am I to say that anything can't happen? Experience may say it is extremely unlikely, that we have no experience with anything like it, and that we should be extremely skeptical. But *impossible* is something quite different from *unlikely*.

Hume said that many reports of miracles came from simple, superstitious people who lived long ago. He said he would listen to miraculous testimony only from an educated person with an impeccable reputation for truth—a person like himself. Some have said Hume would only accept testimony from those who had graduated from an English university.

Hume lost some of his credibility when highly educated physicians with international reputations investigated and credited miraculous healings in France. They were just the kind of witnesses Hume had called for, but Hume was not interested. He knew before investigating that miracles did not happen, no matter who testified that they had. So it is with many skeptics today. They have made up their minds beforehand: Miracles don't happen.

J. E. Renan, author of *The Life of Jesus,* wrote, "Miracles are things which never happen; only credulous people believe they have seen them; you cannot cite a single one which has taken place in presence of witnesses capable of testing it. . . ." And he wrote, "We reject the supernatural for the same reason that we reject the existence of centaurs and hippogriffes; and this reason is, that nobody has ever seen them."[1]

But these assertions are simply not true. Miracles have happened in front of all kinds of people who have testified to them and in some cases have tested them. A thousand witnesses will tell you that they have seen a miracle with their own eyes.

1. Cited in Colin Brown, *Miracles and the Critical Mind* (Grand Rapids, MI: Eerdmans, 1984), 141.

Renan and his friends have a right to be skeptical, but they have no right to claim that miracles are impossible. Science doesn't make that claim. Science tells us to test everything. It doesn't tell us that there's no need to test because we already know the result.

———————

There's a famous story about an Indian prince who entertained officers from the British East India Company. The prince was fascinated by their reports of the world outside his kingdom. He listened intently as they told of factory equipment that could make enormous quantities of cloth in a single day, of bridges that spanned broad rivers, of trains and ships, and of modern guns that could kill at a distance of a mile.

At one report, though, the prince just smiled. He could see that his visitors were pulling his leg when they told him that water in England grew so cold as to turn hard as a rock, sometimes so thick and strong on the surface of ponds that an elephant could walk across without breaking the surface.

The prince knew from experience that such tales were nonsense. Water did not turn into a rock.

The story reminds us that it is very hard to believe what you have never experienced. What we "know" is quite limited. There may be realities beyond our experience that make the impossible seem normal.

It would be very hard to explain to the founders of the American republic—John Adams and George Washington, among others—that business people would routinely fly through the air in a metal tube to destinations halfway around the world; that we would be able to talk to each other and see each other over vast distances using small devices we carry in our pockets; that books and plays would arrive in our homes transmitted invisibly through the air. Any of this—and a great many other common modern realities—would seem like magic or a miracle not so long ago. No doubt many of our ancestors would have thought we were pulling their legs if we told them about radios.

It's odd that with the development of science, we've seen an amazing expansion of what *can* be done matched by a growing assertion about what *cannot*. We can do "miracles" through science and technology, it seems, but the same science and technology are enlisted to tell us that God's miracles are impossible.

In reality, the more we know of the physical universe through science, the more we expand our sense of what might be possible. Science, properly understood, should make us hesitant to declare anything impossible.

I don't know how Jesus walked on water. I don't know whether a physical anomaly made the water congeal under his feet, like the way corn flour solidifies under pressure. Or whether a repellent force came from his feet, lifting him up. Or whether . . . Well, who knows? Since Jesus was physical and the water was physical, I am pretty sure that his miracle could be described in the language of physics, if we knew enough. But we don't.

Most miracles are physical events.[2] They have physical explanations, if they are real. The explanations may or may

2. One might even say that all miracles are physical events, now that we know that thoughts and perceptions in our mind are closely associated with electrical impulses in our brains. A vision, a dream, or a "word of the Lord" happens in our brain and is therefore a physical event.

not be beyond our present understanding, but so what? Lots of things are beyond our present understanding.

I have given a good example already: God miraculously healed Jeff Moore. That healing joyfully shocked all who loved Jeff and powerfully witnessed to the power and goodness of God. It was a wonder and a sign. Without warning, Jeff could walk again. Do I know how? No. Neither do the doctors. Of one thing I am sure: It wasn't a violation of nature. It was the fulfillment of nature—the very thing God intended nature to do.

5

The Semi–Believing Doubter

There's another kind of skeptic whom I find more trouble-some than the materialist we discussed in the last chapter. This sort of skeptic doesn't believe science excludes God. He or she doesn't automatically discount all reports of miracles. This kind of doubter may believe in the possibility of miracles in theory, but in a practical sense, he or she lives as though miracles don't exist. Many Christians fall into this camp. Sometimes I do.

Not long ago I was traveling with my friend Larry, an emergency-room physician who is one of the most idealistic Christians I know. Though he lives and works in Southern California, he seems to spend most of his waking hours (and most of his money) trying to improve health care in Ethiopia. He's cheerful, faithful, and committed in his faith.

Larry and I were on our way to Ethiopia, where I went to report on one of Larry's projects. I had interviewed Jeff Moore only a few weeks before, and the experience was still very much with me.

Curious to know what Larry thought, I related Jeff's story. Just a few sentences into it, though, I realized the story needed all the help I could give it. Hearing Jeff tell what happened is powerful. Hearing me tell it secondhand is less convincing.

I could summarize Jeff's story this way: "Jeff had terribly painful feet, such that he could hardly walk, and then he went to a healing service and the pain disappeared." That's the essence of it, but it sounds too much like a headache that went away, or a traffic jam that mysteriously dissolved. Jeff's story told in summary wouldn't convince anybody that a miracle occurred.

So I told the story as dramatically as I could—the many operations, the loss of hope, the wheelchair, the doctors' resignation. I described Jeff's deadpan personality so that Larry would understand Jeff wasn't the kind of person to talk himself into a miracle.

Even as I told the story in the most convincing detail I could, I felt from Larry's body language that he wasn't really convinced.

Why not? Larry is a dedicated Christian who takes the Bible at face value when it describes miracles. When the Bible says that Jesus turned water into wine, Larry believes it. Furthermore, he believes wholeheartedly that God could still do such an amazing feat. He believes that God is active in the world today.

But as a doctor—as is typical of many doctors—Larry is skeptical about miraculous healing stories. He sees many sick people, and he knows that things happen to them that are hard to predict and explain. Some people get worse unexpectedly. Other people get better. You can't always say why.

Two people may have identical cancers and may receive identical treatment, but one person will get well and the other won't. As far as anyone can tell, it's not a matter of faith or prayer or even attitude. Some bodies fight cancer better than others. People get well for reasons we don't understand.

True, a number of medical studies have found that prayer actually assists healing. But the difference that shows up in studies is subtle, not dramatic, and some studies find no impact. The doctors I know aren't that impressed.

When people heal amazingly, it could be their blood type or their genetics. That's what doctors like Larry often think. They see so much variation in healing that, to them, a spontaneous healing isn't a sign or a wonder.

Larry wasn't denying the possibility that Jeff experienced a miracle. He was just saying that people sometimes heal in the most surprising ways, that the link between mind and body is amazingly strong, and that he wouldn't put too much weight on the claim that God miraculously healed Jeff.

He also doubted whether the issue was that important.

"Isn't the resurrection of Jesus Christ a great enough miracle?" Larry asked me. "If God raised Jesus from the dead after three days in the grave, and demonstrated it in public, why do we need anything else?"

Larry believes our faith should focus on Jesus and his resurrection—a miracle that can't be explained any other way, since dead bodies don't ever come back to life through ordinary events.

Jesus' resurrection is enough for Larry. He isn't looking for miracles to reinforce his faith, and he's not praying for miracles to heal his patients. He's content to apply his skill as a doctor and leave the results in God's good hands.

Larry raises many good points. Maybe the biggest one is a question: How do I know that what healed Jeff is a miracle? If he had grown back an amputated foot, most people would call that miraculous, because such things simply never happen. But in Jeff's case, the timing could be coincidence. Maybe Jeff's feet were finally ready for the healing the doctors had been expecting all along. The mind-body connection could be responsible, too. Maybe those healing prayers triggered thoughts that spurred the body to do what it naturally wants to do—heal.

Healing miracles are often like Jeff's—changes that could have happened through the ordinary healing process.

Larry is also right that, compared to Jesus' resurrection, such "miracles" aren't terribly important events. Nobody's faith depends on the healing of Jeff's foot—except maybe Jeff's and his parents'.

Nevertheless, I don't agree with Larry. I call Jeff's healing a miracle. And I don't think Jesus' resurrection is all we need in the way of miracles. It doesn't stand on its own.

The Bible is very clear about this: Jesus's resurrection was a revolutionary event. When a revolution comes, it introduces a new government, and you will see a difference in the way things are run from that time forward.

That is why Jesus' resurrection doesn't stand alone in the New Testament. During Jesus' life on earth, he healed all kinds of people; those healings demonstrated that the kingdom of God—the new government—had come. Jesus brought power over sickness and evil. That power culminated in the ultimate healing: resurrection.

Nobody had ever overcome death. Even if someone was raised from the grave, like Lazarus, he eventually died. Death had the final word. Death governed all.

Scripture narrates Jesus' resurrection as God's victory over death and evil—a breakthrough that opens a new chapter in human history. Jesus will never die. He lives today. And that resurrection didn't just happen to Jesus; rather, because it happened to him, resurrection will happen to all of us. That's why Paul told the Corinthians, "If there is no resurrection of the dead, then not even Christ has been raised" (1 Corinthians 15:13). The two go together like feather and wing. Jesus lives again after death; *we* will live again after death.

Now we're waiting for our own resurrections, and just as with Jesus' miracles, the signs of the kingdom point toward this victory over death. Healing happened in Jesus' day as a foretaste of his resurrection. Healing happens today as a foretaste of *our* resurrection. Healing and resurrection go together. They did for Jesus. They do for us.

If we don't recognize this linkage, we're left in an uncomfortable position. We don't bother about whether miracles happen in modern times, and we don't argue against skeptics who doubt that miracles happen. And yet, we rightly insist that our lives depend on Jesus' resurrection being real.

When we try to hold that stance—believing in the miracles of the Bible but shrugging skeptically at modern-day miracles—the skepticism of the present day leaks backward. People who disbelieve in miracles in the twenty-first century make the logical leap to doubting miracles in the first century. Pretty soon they start saying that it doesn't matter whether Jesus was really raised from the dead.

In the Lord's Prayer we say, "Your kingdom come; your will be done *on earth as it is in heaven.*" We are asking for miracles every time we pray that prayer. In heaven there is no sickness, no death. We pray for the same to be true on earth. Jesus announced this new regime when he said, "The kingdom of God is at hand," and when he healed people and delivered them from evil spirits. We do the same when we pray for miracles and pray against evil spirits, and when we see God answering our prayers. We are announcing the coming of the kingdom of God.

That doesn't mean that we believe every report of a miracle. It doesn't require Larry to see a sign and a wonder in a physical healing that he, as a doctor, doesn't find that surprising. But it does require that Christians keep an open and honest mind to see what God is doing when he does the unusual.

Most people—most Christians, at any rate—don't want to doubt miracles. They want to believe, even though they quietly think it is pretty unlikely that "impossible" stuff happens or that God actually heals people.

Instead, they define down the word *miracle* until it means almost nothing. They see God in everything that occurs and call everything—a birdsong, a sun shower, a hug—a miracle of God.

That sounds pretty spiritual. If you listen carefully, though, you'll often see they're taking God *out* of miracles. For them, a miracle is something inspirational. It's a pick-me-up.

Here are a few uses of the word *miracle* I found on a quick scan of the Internet:

> *Miracle* is a 2004 film about the 1980 USA Olympic hockey team that won a gold medal against Russia.
>
> Miracle is the name of the Fort Myers, Florida, minor-league baseball team.
>
> "The miracle of friendship can be spoken without words. . . ."

"The child must know that he is a miracle. . . ."
"All of my days are miracles."
"Life itself is the miracle of miracles."
"Ingenuity, plus courage, plus work, equals miracles."
"Don't believe in miracles—depend on them."

In these definitions, *miracle* applies to anything marvelous, inspirational, or valuable. Friends are miracles. So are rainbows. So is life itself. When we use *miracle* in this cuddly, inspirational way, there's no reason to bring God into the picture. A "miracle" is the equivalent of an emoticon. It may be a wonder, but it's not a sign.

Leif Enger's novel, *Peace Like a River*, puts it this way:

> For too long [the word *miracle*] has been used to characterize things or events that, though pleasant, are entirely normal. Peeping chicks at Easter time, spring generally, a clear sunrise after an overcast week—a miracle, people say, as if they've been educated from greeting cards. I'm sorry, but nope. Such things are worth our notice every day of the week, but to call them miracles evaporates the strength of the word.[1]

If I say those aren't miracles, it's because I want to preserve the startling character of real miracles. God does beautiful and inspiring things every day, but only very occasionally does he do something so unusual and so meaningful it seizes our attention and makes us cry out in praise. I believe God does such things still, as a sign of his coming kingdom.

In everyday life, most Christians get along just fine without ever thinking about God's involvement in the physical realm. Headache? They take aspirin. Appendicitis? They rush to the

---

1. Leif Enger, *Peace Like a River* (New York: Grove Press, 2001), 3.

emergency room. They take the healing claims of televange-lists with a dose of salt.

Only in times of crisis do they truly hope for miracles. Faced with cancer, they go for chemotherapy, but when that fails, they cry out to God for healing. Occasionally a speaker in church raises their hopes, and they take a new stab at living with an expectation of miracles. Maybe they hear of someone like Jeff being healed and get their hopes up.

But as my pastor says, "They don't live there." They soon fall back into ordinary life, claiming to believe in God's ac-tivity but failing to live or think as though they did. Maybe they pray for God "to do something amazing," but they don't really expect it to happen.

Hey, I'm not criticizing. I do the same thing.

What I call the semi-charismatic mind-set claims to believe one thing about God and lives out another. Churches may pray for people by name, but they don't actually expect to see any results. In fact, they get quite expert at telling people not to expect too much when they pray.

A doctor like Larry says that we can't be sure Jeff's healing was supernatural. After all, bodies have amazing and unpre-dictable healing properties. What happened can probably be explained physically, even if we don't know exactly how.

To which I answer: However God touched Jeff's feet, he had to do it physically. I don't doubt a bit that God used some natural process in Jeff's body to take the pain away.

But that doesn't diminish the miracle. Jeff is healed! He was instantaneously healed in response to prayer! His heal-ing startled and amazed everybody who cared about him, including his doctors! He is praising God for what happened! The pain is gone!

All healing is from God and is worthy of our praise and thanks. When one of those healings is medically startling and closely associated with prayer, it's a special event, the kind we call miraculous, and a reason for a greater outpouring of praise and thanks. Or do you think Jeff and his family should just shrug their shoulders at this extraordinary gift and say, "Huh. How about that? I couldn't walk, and now I can. I guess that's a good deal for me, but I have no idea how it happened or what it means."

Of course not. They know how it happened and what it means. God has his hands all over it. He has given them a wonderful and stunning gift, a sign and a wonder.

———

When I was just out of college, I worked for a small Christian publishing company run by an aggressively charismatic boss. He wanted me to join him in his Pentecostal way of thinking. Regarding healing miracles, he pointed me to Psalm 103:2–3, which reads, "Praise the Lord, my soul, and forget not all his benefits—who forgives all your sins and heals all your diseases."

My boss believed God's healing power was available to anyone at any time, and in this Scripture he saw that availability confirmed. God forgives all our sins if we ask him, and just as surely he heals all our diseases. Ask and you will receive.

Since I hadn't seen healing miracles, I had a hard time dealing with this interpretation. As I pondered it, though, I realized the psalm was true in my experience. Throughout my life I had been sick hundreds of times. In every case, God healed me. He has healed all my diseases.

It's true of almost everyone. God has given us bodies that are wonderfully prone to heal. I marvel at it. If you scratch the paint on your car, the scratch will be repaired only through a painstaking process of sanding and painting. Not so your finger. You don't have to do anything but wait. In a few days the red wound will begin to harden and new skin will grow. A scab will form, then eventually fall off. In a month the finger will be as good as new—you won't see the slightest sign that any injury occurred.

Is this mechanical? Yes, in a sense it is. Doctors can explain how it happens in great detail. It is also supernatural. God is closely involved with the process—as close as a potter forming a clay pot, as personal as a plasterer repairing a wall. Our bodies heal, and God is the healer. Not every healing is a miracle. In fact, healing miracles are quite rare, almost by definition, but every healing comes from God, and there are a lot of them to praise him for.

I can join the psalmist and say, "He forgives all my sins and he heals all my diseases."

Of course, someone may respond, "What about people who aren't healed? What about those who die of cancer?"

As soon as you say that God is involved in everything that happens, you open up a host of questions. How can you believe in a good God if he allowed my child to die? If he allowed slaves to suffer? If he permitted the Holocaust? Was he there and standing by?

For many people, these are the deepest objections to miracles. If God gets credit for every healing, will he also take credit for every suffering?

These kinds of questions have been asked many times through the centuries, and it would take more than one book to summarize the many theological and philosophical attempts at answers. I would like to make a few observations, though:

1. Scripture recognizes these questions as legitimate. The book of Job is dedicated to exploring them, and many of the Psalms powerfully articulate their emotions. Jesus himself cried out, "My God, my God, why have you forsaken me?" If Jesus asked it, so can we.

2. The Bible usually lets these questions stand unanswered. While the questions are legitimate, an explanation is not offered. It may be that we simply cannot grasp what is involved in the answer any more than a child can follow a complex philosophical discussion. That is what God's response to Job implies when God demands to know "Where were you when I laid the earth's foundation?" (Job 38:4) and "Do you give the horse its strength?" (Job 39:19).

3. God does not dodge responsibility for our suffering. It is his universe, and he never suggests that anything is beyond his control. But he points to the future. In the end, the Bible says there will be total and comprehensive obedience to Jesus Christ, and there will be no suffering, no pain, no death, and no injustice. But until we reach that day, we live by faith. That is to say, God asks us to trust him even when his management of the universe doesn't make sense to us.

4. Signs and wonders are one way that God reaches out to us and suggests that the "normal" is not the "eternal." Joy and relief are coming, even if they remain scattered and mostly hidden. Miracles are God's messengers to us, not necessarily suggesting that healing is available to everybody at all times, but that *it will be someday because God has promised to make it so.*

A miracle is a glimmering of what will be. It is a sign, pointing not to itself, but to God and to the resurrection future that God will bring. As we try to investigate miracles, we need to focus on what they say to us. Miracles are like signals from a distant ship. We may see them dimly through the fog, and we may not even be sure just what we see, but they signal another world coming to join our own—"the New Jerusalem, coming down out of heaven from God" (Revelation 21:2).

We sometimes think that seeing a miracle will dispel all doubt for all time, but experience shows that isn't so. The evidence never compels belief. Miracles didn't convince everybody in Jesus' time, and they don't today. Miracles are rare events. They are not "proof." You can't ask for and expect a repeat performance; that comes only with the next life.

Let no skeptic say, however, that miracles are impossible. Improbable, always, but not impossible.

And let no one say that miracles are unimportant. In isolation, perhaps they are. What does it matter that Jeff's feet were healed, except to Jeff? But miracles are not isolated events. Rather, they are signals of a larger trend. They point to something beyond themselves. They point to a future reality. They point to a present God.

6

The Old Testament and Its Miracles

In regular life, miracles are rare, but in the Bible, they hit you like an avalanche. The life of Jesus—one miracle after another. The exodus from Egypt, the conquest of the Promised Land, the days of Noah, the life of Elijah. Miracles cluster like apples on a tree, like stars in the sky.

Some people read of these miracles and get drawn in. They long to see God and experience his power. The Bible's miracles promise that they can.

Others read and grow skeptical. Life isn't like that. Is the Bible really reporting the truth? Perhaps the reports of miracles are exaggerated, and if they are exaggerated, who can say other parts of the Bible are reliable? The miracles of the Bible cause these people to doubt the Bible.

When you look more closely at the Bible, though, you discover that the issue is not as stark as it may at first seem. Yes, dramatic miracles happen—and no amount of revisionist editing can get rid of them. But miracles in the Bible are actually quite unusual. If you start at the time of Abraham and follow through to the time of Jesus, you cover about two thousand years. In those two millennia of Bible history, only a few periods were studded with miracles. They tended to come in clusters. The exodus, the early prophets, and the time of Jesus produced the vast majority of the miracles. Together they cover approximately 140 years—perhaps 7 percent of the two-thousand-year total.

In the other 93 percent—including the years of Abraham, Isaac, Jacob, and Joseph; the time of the writing prophets like Isaiah, Amos, and Jeremiah; the period of David and Solomon; the Babylonian captivity; and the return to the Promised Land—few miracles are mentioned.

It's quite possible other miracles just didn't get written down. The Bible is not preoccupied with miracles. It tells about the people God chose and how he set out to redeem them. Clearly, miracles come and go, but God's salvation is a constant force, always in operation on every page of Scripture.

Some people think great faith and great miracles always go together. If you don't see miracles, they say, it must be because you lack faith. So they may say of a certain church, "They preach the Bible, but the power is missing."

The Bible would suggest that this is a mistaken interpretation. Otherwise, we would have to conclude that power was missing for David. For Isaiah. For Jeremiah. For Nehemiah. They saw few if any miracles, and nowhere does Scripture suggest that this represents a failure on their part.

Have you noticed that miracles are rare in the sophisticated, educated, and wealthier countries of the world, while in the slums of Africa or Latin America, in the house churches of

China or India, we hear many miraculous reports? Does this mean that the Spirit is most alive in the miracle places? That the Western churches lack faith? That could be true, but the Bible would give you no reason to think so based simply on the count of miracles. Were the Israelites whom Moses dragged out of Egypt more faithful than the Israelites who left Babylon to rebuild Jerusalem? One would doubt it, but the Exodus Israelites saw many spectacular miracles, and the Israelites who restored Jerusalem saw none.

We are mistaken to see miracles as a divine stamp of approval, and lack of miracles as a divine judgment. Sometimes, in fact, the Bible speaks of the craving for miracles as a *lack* of faith. Jesus himself suggests that, as we'll see.

We ought to consider miracles as one instrument that God sometimes uses to help his people. They serve God's purposes, but they are not an end in themselves.

THE CREATION STORIES: GENESIS 1–11

Remember what a miracle is: something God does in a highly unusual way, seizing our attention and communicating something about God's nature and purpose. A miracle is a sign and a wonder.[1]

---

1. Physician David Graham prefers the American College Dictionary's definition for miracle: "An effect in the physical world which surpasses all known human or natural powers and is therefore ascribed to supernatural agency." I think that definition is too narrow.

In the first place, there is no reason to think that most miracles "surpass all known human or natural powers." When Jesus healed Peter's mother-in-law of a fever (Luke 4:38–39) were unknown powers involved? I think not. The miracle had to do with timing, not "unnatural powers." Even highly unusual miracles may not involve "unknown powers." Some creatures walk on water just as Jesus did; some creatures regenerate limbs. Quite possibly the same forces that propel the "normal" events might propel the unusual.

By that definition, all the stories of the early chapters of Genesis are miraculous, though we don't usually think of them in that category. The creation of the universe can never be anything but extraordinary! It happens only once, and it conveys the mastery of God, his splendor and his beauty.

These beginnings set our fundamental relationship to God: art to artist, creature to creator. In love and in power God made this beautiful world, including human beings, and he called it good.

Cambridge biochemist Denis Alexander, however, points out that the Bible never refers to the creation events with miracle language. They are wondrous acts of power, but they are also the foundation of all "normal" events. They set in place the natural forces—gravity, solar energy, biological diversity—that rule everyday life. They are the foundation of normalcy. Perhaps for that reason the language of miracle isn't used to describe them. (Besides, nobody was present to witness them, and thus experience surprise.)

Almost immediately after the creation, God's wondrous creatures turn to destruction. That unleashes what must surely be called "miracle"—miracles of judgment. God so loved the world he created, yet he judges the world in a terrible, killing flood. He destroys human plans by scrambling human communication at Babel. God does destructive miracles. These are signs and wonders.

Secondly, the definition offers a hint of the "natural-supernatural" dichotomy, and thus "the God of the gaps." It suggests that if we don't know how it happened, it must be God's supernatural activity. But the natural and the supernatural are not separate. Everything is both natural and supernatural at the same time.

When we come to understand the physical process behind a miracle, it does not mean God was not involved. If you could explain exactly what happened to the bones and the nerves in Jeff Moore's feet, I would still call what happened a miracle.

God's acts in Genesis 1–11 are distinct from most of the rest of the Bible in that they affect the whole world. The creation is the story of the whole universe. Adam and Eve are the parents of all people. The flood of Noah judges the entire world, and Babel changes all human language.

THE PATRIARCHS: ABRAHAM AND HIS OFFSPRING

After this global beginning, miracles in the Bible become more local. If you've read Genesis, you know what a dramatic change comes in the twelfth chapter. Suddenly, instead of a global view, just one desert nomad comes into focus.

If Hollywood made this film, it would start with a view of the watery globe, a blue marble streaked with clouds. Then the camera would zoom down to a panorama of the Middle East, and then zero in still further to a single tent pitched under a desert sky. Let me introduce you to Abraham, the father of Israel. Here is the blessing of the world, disguised as a nobody.

Abraham, Isaac, Jacob, and Joseph: Through these four men (and their brothers and sisters and wives and uncles and cousins and servants), God reestablishes his grip on the human race. He does it with very few interventions that we would recognize as miracles. We see God's involvement mainly through his presence, as he speaks and appears in visions, repeating the same promises again and again. Sometimes he provides in extraordinary ways, using what seems to be coincidence. For example, God tells Abraham to sacrifice his son, Isaac, and then at the last moment tells him to stop. When he looks around, Abraham sees a ram, stuck by its horns in the bushes, ready as a substitute for Isaac. That's a miracle, but much subtler than what God will do through Moses years later.

The birth of Isaac is also a miracle, coming as it does when both Abraham and Sarah are very old. God had promised them a son, and he had predicted the son's coming after a long, long wait, so there was no doubt this unusual birth was God's doing.

The destruction of Sodom was clearly a miracle of judgment. God also inflicted blindness on the evil men seeking to kill Lot and rape his guests, another miracle of judgment. On Abraham and Sarah's behalf, God brought a disease on two different sets of neighbors who took Sarah into their harem.

Isaac and Jacob, so far as we know, witnessed no miracles, though Jacob had mystical dreams and encounters with God.

Joseph was involved with miraculous doings when he was able to interpret Pharaoh's dreams and predict seven years of good harvest followed by seven years of famine. When it came to his kidnapping and later his imprisonment on false charges, however, no miracles came. Nor did God provide food to his extended family during the seven years of famine, except through the crops that grew in Egypt through ordinary means.

The patriarchs saw few signs and wonders. More commonly, they encountered God as he spoke to them or gave them visions. Most of what God did for them, he did invisibly: He protected them and blessed them and enabled them to prosper. Their neighbors sometimes realized that Abraham's family had a special relationship with a powerful God, but that was because God provided for them, not because signs and wonders were sprinkled around them.

FOUR HUNDRED YEARS IN EGYPT, FOLLOWED BY EXODUS

We know very little about the generations who lived in Egypt, except that they gradually went from honored guests to oppressed slaves. We know of no miracles. From what we can gather, Jacob's offspring retained very little connection to the godly heritage of Abraham. They seem to have forgotten the great promises that God made to him and his descendants.

God took the initiative. At first his actions were private—saving Moses' life by letting him be adopted by Pharaoh's daughter, then speaking to him from a burning bush and calling him into leadership.

From that point on, however, miracles were public and unmistakable. God gave Moses the ability to do miraculous signs, proving to Pharaoh that God had sent him. He could turn his staff into a snake and back again; he could contract leprosy and then be cured; he could turn water into blood.

And even more spectacular miracles followed. First came miracles of judgment, as Moses and Aaron pronounced plague after plague on the stubborn Pharaoh. Then came the parting of the waters of the Red Sea, the cloud of fire, the manna from heaven, the water from a rock, and other amazing events.

The parting of the Red Sea is worthy of note because it clearly involved both natural and supernatural causes working together. "Then Moses stretched out his hand over the sea, and all that night the Lord drove the sea back with a strong east wind and turned it into dry land" (Exodus 14:21). God did it; a wind did it. Which was it? It was both.

God gave his law to Moses in a spectacular, fire-and-thunder ceremony on Mount Sinai. He confirmed Aaron's leadership by having his staff bud, blossom, and produce almonds overnight. He punished the guilty in miracles of judgment, even to the extent of opening a hole in the ground that swallowed up a rebellious clan. (See Numbers 16.) He stopped Balaam from opposing Israel by making his donkey speak.

When you read about the Exodus, you never get the sense that God did miracles in response to the people's faith or virtue. Quite the contrary. The Israelites showed themselves to be forgetful, ungrateful, quarrelsome, and fearful. This was a golden era for Israel, but they were not a golden people. Miracles reflect on God and what he does, not the people on the receiving end.

One of the Israelites' worst moments came precisely because they demanded a miracle. Understandably thirsty in the desert, they demanded that God provide water, and God answered their prayer miraculously, making water come out of a rock (Numbers 17:1–7). But as Psalm 95 declares, he was angry at them for forty years because they had no business ordering him around. "Putting God to the test" showed a lack of faith.

THE KINGS AND THE PROPHETS

Israel finally came to the Promised Land under Joshua's leadership, and miracles continued as God gave them victory over the inhabitants. The walls of Jericho miraculously fell down and allowed Joshua's terrified army to occupy the city and conquer its inhabitants (Joshua 6:20). Later, the sun stopped to prolong a battle with the Amorites. God sent giant hailstones to fall on the enemy, killing them (Joshua 10).

But as soon as the Israelites settled into their new home, miracles mostly stopped. The book of Judges is filled with spectacular battles, but few miracles. (Gideon was a major exception to the rule.)

For five hundred years after the time of the Judges, Israel was ruled by kings. Saul came first, quickly followed by David and Solomon. Thirty-nine kings followed, most of them bad. Not one of them, good or bad, was known for miracles.

In response to terrible leadership, God sent prophets, men who spoke for God. Much of what they said warned the kings and their people to change their ways or face the consequences, as the prophets reminded Israel of the high standards God expected of them. Sometimes the prophets predicted the future, but they did that relatively seldom. They were God's messengers, sent to the powers appointed by God in order to set them right. Prophets were not known for miracles, either.

There is one major exception. During a period of about eighty years, miracles happened frequently through the prophets Elijah and Elisha. These two addressed a string of very bad kings: Ahab, Ahaziah, Joram, Jehu, Hehoahaz, and Jehoash. Ahab was arguably the worst king Israel ever had, egged on by his sinister wife, Jezebel.

Under these kings, Israel fell under the influence of Baal, a cruel local god. Elijah and Elisha fought (mostly with words, but sometimes with other weapons) to preserve Israel's faithfulness to the God of Abraham.

Through miraculous interventions, God enabled Elijah and Elisha to survive a very threatening environment. Ravens fed Elijah in hiding. A widow's jars of oil and flour kept providing food in a time of famine. The widow's son was miraculously healed. Then God sent fire down from heaven when Elijah confronted the prophets of Baal on Mount Carmel.

Elisha in his turn did spectacular miracles, including healing a foreign general from leprosy, the most feared disease of that era. Through many heroic confrontations, these prophets lived by God's miracles. (And so, in a much less heroic confrontation, did Jonah.)

In Moses and Joshua's time, liberation was at stake—the journey from slavery to freedom. For Elijah and Elisha, survival was at stake. They had few allies to call on for help, so God came to the rescue.

During the rest of this five-hundred-year royal period, though, almost no miracles were recorded. Some very great leaders appeared: David, Isaiah, and Jeremiah, for a start. David was a man of extraordinary passion for God—a poet and a musician as well as a military general and a king. He showed great faith, from the time when he fought the giant Goliath to the moment when he refused to kill Saul even though he had him in his power. God helped him, God provided for him, and God protected him, but God did not do miracles for him. (His victory over Goliath is sometimes thought of as a miracle, but nothing in the story suggests that God worked in unusual ways. Slingshots can kill, if you're a good shot.)

The same could be said of Jeremiah—a prophet who complained bitterly against his calling—who was imprisoned and very nearly murdered for his faith. Though God affirmed Jeremiah as his chosen instrument, he did not protect him by miraculous means.

Isaiah and Jeremiah and all the prophets pronounced inspired messages that came from God. They sometimes made accurate predictions about the future. One might call these messages miraculous, but they were not visible (they happened in the minds and hearts of the prophets), nor were they wonders to those who heard them. Only much later would people think of the prophets' words with awe. At the time, they mainly inspired irritation and consternation.

THE EXILE AND RETURN

The Old Testament's final period shows Israel at its worst and its best. The Babylonian captivity came after repeated warnings from God. He had told them through the prophets that he would abandon them if they could not live up to their calling. They didn't listen, and the nation slowly went downhill. Finally, God allowed the Assyrians to capture the North and take its people into exile, and then the Babylonians to take the South, including Jerusalem. Israel's kings were assassinated or taken captive. The temple was destroyed. Utter ruin came as the survivors were carted off to foreign lands. Psalm 137:1 captures the emotional devastation: "By the waters of Babylon we sat and wept. . . ."

For approximately seventy years they lived as captive foreigners, and the books of Daniel, Ezekiel, and Esther chronicle a few faithful lives in exile. In the case of Daniel, several outstanding miracles occurred. Three of his friends survived a fire meant to kill them. Daniel spent the night untouched by a pride of hungry lions. A prophecy was written on a wall by an invisible presence.

Eventually a new empire came to power, allowing Israelites to voluntarily return to their Promised Land. It was not an easy journey, and only a minority took it. Criminals and bandits were rampant, and there was no security available. Yet several waves of Israelites returned to rebuild—first their houses and the city wall, and soon the temple. They were too poor to rebuild anything as magnificent as what had been destroyed, but in a smaller, plainer temple they began to worship God again in the way they had been taught under Moses.

During Israel's worst times of destruction, there were no miracles of judgment. God used foreign armies to punish Israel; he didn't send fire from heaven to punish or protect them. And during Israel's best times of return to the Promised Land, God used hard work and ingenuity to rebuild. He didn't miraculously provide.

If you believe the Bible, this survey of the Old Testament is bound to emphasize the reality of God's miraculous power. There's no way around the astonishing displays that occurred. You can't finesse the parting of the Red Sea or the fire that came from heaven to burn up Elijah's offering.

At the same time, you must see that God doesn't always do miracles. Even his best and most faithful people may know nothing of signs and wonders. Rather, God does miracles at times of his choosing.

With that background, we turn to the brief period of the New Testament, when God's miracles again came in a downpour.

7

The Miracles of the New Testament

God did miracles in Jesus' life. In the accounts known as the Gospels—Matthew, Mark, Luke, and John—we read of healings, exorcisms, and other wonders on almost every page. No other period of the Bible is so spangled with miracles, except the Exodus.

These two periods, the Exodus and the Incarnation, form the Bible's two dramatic acts of redemption. In act one, God freed his people from political and social slavery; in act two, God freed his people from the slavery of sin and death. (Though they still sinned and still died, they had joined an exodus march into a kingdom that would put an end to both.) In each case, God's power was very visible.

But one important difference should be noted. In the Exodus, miracles were public spectacles aimed at a national audience. News didn't have to spread by word of mouth; tens of thousands of people had only to open their eyes to witness spectacular signs and wonders. The plagues of Egypt affected the whole nation. Frogs were everywhere; hail killed cattle in every field. Later, when manna came from heaven, every Israelite gathered it and ate. Moses' miracles were aimed at nations.

The miracles of Jesus' life were almost always for a smaller audience, sometimes just for the single individual seeking help. Jesus made no attempt to reach masses of people with his miracles. In fact, at many points Jesus tried to keep news of his miracles from spreading.

"Jesus said to [the man with leprosy], 'See that you don't tell anyone' " (Matthew 8:4); "As they were coming down the mountain [of Transfiguration], Jesus instructed them, 'Don't tell anyone what you have seen' " (Matthew 17:9); "Jesus commanded [those who had seen his miraculous healings] not to tell anyone" (Mark 7:36). There are many other examples.

It's a strikingly different approach. Imagine Moses, standing for hours with his hands held high, prompting the strong winds that blew back the Red Sea, then urging those around him, "Don't tell anybody!" What a joke that would be! Everybody knew!

But Jesus said those words often. News of his miracles got passed around nonetheless, and his reputation spread, but from the beginning of his life on earth to the end, people responded to him on an individual basis. Signs and wonders marked his birth, and men came from great distances to honor him, but in his own hometown, few knew his significance. His resurrection, similarly, was witnessed by his followers, but his new life wasn't broadcast with the idea of national exposure. The risen Jesus did not speak from the steps of the temple. He did not call on Pilate.

That same quality has marked Jesus' miracles ever since. They are not typically public spectacles. I have asked many people whether they have seen a miracle, and a surprising number tell me they have. Most have seen just one—but one that was, in their minds, incontrovertible. And often when I listen to them, I have to nod and say, "Yes, if it happened the way you describe, it really does sound like a miracle."

For example, a friend, Gary, described a very trying time thirty years ago. He was a young Christian, and his girlfriend had just broken up with him. She had left him twice before, and they had gotten back together, but this time seemed terribly final. Gary was devastated; his girlfriend had helped him grow through his earliest days as a Christian, and he was quite emotionally dependent on her. All his inner feelings cried out.

As they drove away in separate cars from their college campus, two freeway ramps diverged. Gary watched his girlfriend's taillights go one way while he went the other. The thought entered his mind: *Just like our lives, headed in different directions.* At the very instant this thought entered his head, a meteor streaked across the sky, broke into two, and sent two diverging trails across the horizon. For Gary, that was the clearest and most miraculous revelation possible. In a very shaky time of his life, when he lacked confidence that God would take care of him, that meteor reassured him that God was in control of the universe and was directing his life. It was too great a coincidence to be a coincidence. It meant the world to Gary. But he almost never told anybody, because what would it mean to them?

Another friend, David, had just graduated from college and indicated to his denomination that he felt called to become

95

a minister. Before he headed to seminary, he was assigned to help out in a church over the summer. One week when the pastor was away, David, green as could be, was in charge. He got a phone call that sent panic into his soul. Ed, one of the church's most beloved elders, had been suddenly diagnosed with brain cancer. The surgeon wanted to operate immediately.

David knew he was in over his head, but he proceeded to follow the course he thought was right. He contacted the church elders and told them that he thought they should gather to pray for Ed. Would they convene at Ed's bedside before the surgery?

They did so. David had brought some olive oil, which he used to anoint Ed, and together they asked God to heal him. Then Ed went into the operating room for a ten-hour surgery. David was relieved that he had done his part, but it hardly occurred to him that Ed might be healed.

But Ed was healed. When the surgeon opened up his brain, he could find no cancer at all—nothing. He was completely flummoxed by the discovery. And my friend David, who has seen few other miracles in the forty years since, was encouraged to learn that when we pray, God listens and acts.

Both those examples seem to me to be miracles. They were utterly surprising and unexpected. They created a sense of awe and wonder. And they functioned as signs pointing to God. But in neither case were they of wide public interest. The stories would find deep appreciation among close friends and family, but they would hardly make the evening news.

Most of Jesus' miracles were more public than either of those examples, as many took place with crowds all around.

Still, as public proof of his Lordship, the miracles left something to be desired. If Jesus wanted to prove something, he should have behaved more like Moses. Rather than quietly turn water into wine at a wedding, he should have made the Jordan River flow with wine. Rather than providing bread once to five thousand, he should have given it to the whole nation at designated feeding stations. Instead of healing those few who could get to him, he should have stood on a mountain and waved his hands, healing thousands simultaneously.

Today as then, God's miracles are not the kinds of acts of power that work as public proof. If God wanted to prove something, he wouldn't straighten legs or heal brain tumors on the occasional individual. He wouldn't make painful feet stop hurting. He would wipe out cancer completely in Peoria. He would turn the Mississippi green on St. Patrick's Day.

But he doesn't do that. I'm not saying he can't or that he won't, but as a matter of fact, he doesn't. He didn't do that kind of spectacle when he lived on earth in bodily form, either. His miracles were consistently the kind you can miss if you aren't looking, and the kind you can doubt even if you were there to witness them yourself. Even the resurrection. Matthew 28:17 says, "When [the eleven disciples] saw [the resurrected Jesus], they worshiped him; *but some doubted*" (emphasis mine).

That prompts the question: If he wasn't trying to prove his Lordship to the world through signs and wonders, what was Jesus trying to do?

The New Testament records about twenty-two occasions when Jesus healed someone miraculously. In addition, on multiple occasions, a gospel describes Jesus healing considerable but unknown numbers of people, as in Luke 4:40: "At sunset, the people brought to Jesus all who had various kinds of sickness, and laying his hands on each one, he healed them."

Many of these healings were closely related to the exorcism of evil spirits. Jesus' miracles overcame powerfully dark forces, and, in fact, all of Jesus' work fought against the power of evil in the world, sometimes referred to as Satan, and sometimes referred to as Death.

On nine occasions Jesus did miracles that showed his control over his creation. He calmed a storm, he walked on water, he turned water into wine, he orchestrated a huge catch of fish.

Finally, Jesus restored to life three different individuals who had died: Jairus' daughter, the son of a widow at Nain, and Jesus' friend Lazarus. These could be considered healings, but they are a particular kind of healing.

Most of these miracles were prompted by simple compassion. We easily forget how helpless people were in the ages before modern medicine. I thought of this recently when I interviewed women with fistulas in Dembi Dollo, Ethiopia, a remote spot near the Sudan border. The women's stories were all roughly the same. They went into labor in a remote area far from a hospital. Their babies were too big for the birth canal, and the women labored for a minimum of three days. On the third day, their babies stopped moving—they had died. But it was usually more days before the dead child could come out, sometimes in a dismembered state.

And then the mother's suffering had only begun, because during labor, the baby's head had pushed so hard and so long on her pelvis that it killed tissue. The woman healed, but with holes that leaked urine and feces. She couldn't help dribbling and stinking. Usually she was very shortly deserted by her husband and ostracized by her community. She lived alone, indoors. It was an awful, hopeless life, unless she could get to a hospital that did fistula surgery.

I listened, stunned, to these women's stories. Their suffering was almost unimaginable. They had begun one day with the hope of bringing a new baby into the world. That dream had become, for them, a nightmare.

And I realized that their condition was not unique. All through human history, women have suffered from fistulas. New York City opened a women's hospital devoted to fistula repair in 1855. It closed in 1928.

In Jesus' day there were no hospitals that did fistula surgery, so undoubtedly, some such desperate women came to him. And he healed them.

Fistulas were only one of many intractable problems. In those days, if your child got a fever, you could only wait to see whether it would kill him. Broken legs, an infected wound, a bad cough—you could only wait and see. People died of such things all the time. They were utterly helpless with ravages of sickness that we now treat routinely. Jesus felt for people oppressed by disease. He could help them, so he did. He was a compassionate man.

"A man with leprosy came to him and begged him on his knees, 'If you are willing, you can make me clean.' Jesus was indignant. He reached out his hand and touched the man. 'I am willing,' he said. 'Be clean!' " (Mark 1:40–41).

Leprosy is a treatable disease today; in Jesus' day, *he* was the only treatment.

"Then Jesus asked them, 'Which is lawful on the Sabbath: to do good or to do evil, to save life or to kill?' But they remained silent. He looked around at them in anger and, deeply distressed at their stubborn hearts, said to the man, 'Stretch out your hand.' He stretched it out, and his hand was completely restored" (Mark 3:4–5).

Note that Jesus could not send the man for hand surgery, as we could today.

"When the Lord saw her [a widow whose only son had died], his heart went out to her and he said, 'Don't cry.' Then he went up and touched the bier they were carrying him on . . . 'Young man, I say to you, get up!' The dead man sat up and began to talk, and Jesus gave him back to his mother" (Luke 7:13–15).

Jesus wept over his friend Lazarus when he visited his tomb.

Then as now, there was no treatment for death.

Jesus reacted with compassion for desperate people. He did healing miracles because no good medical alternatives existed. Without a miracle, these people had little or no hope.

This situation has changed. If we want to heal desperate people as much as Jesus did, we should train doctors. They are very effective at alleviating suffering. God in his gracious love for the world has enabled the development of medicine, and we should thank him for it. The inventor of penicillin healed a thousand times as many people as Jesus ever did. So did those who discovered the vaccines for smallpox and polio. Medicine has taken on a vast share of the burden of helpless, desperately sick people. Jesus is not in competition with that; he loves medicine. So should we, if we care about sick people.

For the sake of compassion, we don't need miracles as much as the people in Jesus' day, and that is a very good thing.

Nevertheless, compassion is not out-of-date. Despite modern medicine, Jeff Moore couldn't walk. Despite great advances in cancer treatments, young mothers die of brain tumors. Despite huge expenditures on medical research, those with Parkinson's have no cure. If we care for them, we should pray for their miraculous healing.

***

Jesus' healings weren't just from compassion. He also responded to faith: to the faith of a centurion (Luke 7); to the faith of two blind men (Matthew 9:29); to the faith of friends who brought a crippled man to him (Luke 5:20); to the faith of a woman who pushed forward in a crowd to touch his robe (Luke 8:28); to the faith of a Canaanite woman who wouldn't take no for an answer (Matthew 15:28). He loved to help people who believed that God could do miracles, who sought them out from Jesus.

Jesus' disciples once asked him why they had failed to cast a demon out of a self-destructive boy. (Jesus did it in a moment.) Jesus explained, "Because you have so little faith" (Matthew 17:20). He told them that if they had as much faith as a mustard seed, nothing would be impossible for them.

Jesus was a man of perfect faith, and he wanted others to share that faith. He knew the kingdom of God would break in as they did. Faith and prayer are (or should be) closely related. Faith in God leads us to ask for miraculous help.

Once, when Jesus healed a man who was paralyzed, he explicitly explained why he did it: "I want you to know that the Son of Man has authority on earth to forgive sins" (Luke

5:24). He used a visible, tangible sign to show his authority to do something invisible and spiritual. He healed the man so that people would recognize his greater ministry of forgiving sins. As Hebrews 2:4 puts it, "God also testified to [Jesus' salvation] by signs, wonders and various miracles."

Most of the time, though, Jesus didn't explain why he healed or did miracles. He just did them. Jesus taught his disciples to pray these words to their Father in heaven: "Your will be done on earth as it is in heaven." Jesus provided on earth the resources that never go missing in heaven. He healed. (Nobody is sick in heaven.) He provided food for hungry people. (Nobody goes hungry in heaven.) He gave orders to natural forces—storms, for example—that raged out of control. Jesus did what came naturally to him, following the direction of his Father in heaven. For him, there was nothing extraordinary about his signs and wonders. They were normal.

He wanted them to be normal for his disciples, too. He gave them authority to heal and cast out demons when he sent them out on a mission—once to the twelve, and later to a larger group of seventy-two. They succeeded; the seventy-two returned from their mission with joy (Luke 10:17).

Nowhere in the Bible does Jesus or anyone else give lessons in how to heal or cast out demons. Many students of the Bible have pored over it, trying to learn from what Jesus did, but they don't discover an operating manual, or even any standard practices. Sometimes Jesus laid hands on people, sometimes he rubbed mud on them, sometimes he healed from across town. Sometimes he gave orders verbally to a disease or a demon; sometimes he declared healing to the person in need; sometimes he prayed, and other times he did not. If there is a right way to go about these things, it is difficult to get it from the Bible.

So it was among his first followers, too. The letters of Paul, though they give many practical instructions on many topics, say nothing about how to practice miracles. James is the only one of the Bible's letter-writers to instruct on healing. (He says to have the elders anoint with oil and pray.)

So if you want to be an expert miracle worker, don't expect the New Testament to tell you how. It is not an instruction manual.

The New Testament tells about Jesus. Jesus did miracles. They were absolutely an essential part of his ministry, inaugurating the kingdom of God in our world. He fully expected his disciples to do the same kind of work, and they did. After he was gone, they carried on with healings and casting out evil spirits just as he had done.

This still leaves a question: If signs and wonders were normal for Jesus and his disciples, what were they meant to accomplish? They didn't do away with the troubles of the world, or change earth into heaven. They didn't provide universal proof of God's power the way Moses' miracles did for the Egyptians. They were seen by only a small fraction of those living in Palestine, and they helped an even smaller fraction.

At first glance, Jesus seems to have contradictory ideas about miracles. He criticized the Pharisees and Sadducees when they demanded that he prove himself by doing miracles. "A wicked and adulterous generation asks for a miraculous sign!" he told them (Matthew 12:39 NIV). He said only the sign of Jonah would be given—the prophet's three days in the belly of a whale prefiguring Jesus' death and resurrection.

The crowds following him wanted to see a sign "that we may see it and believe you" (John 6:30). They reminded Jesus that Moses had provided manna. Surely Jesus could do so, as well.

In response, Jesus spoke of God giving them "the true bread from heaven." When they asked for it, he said, "I am the bread of life. Whoever comes to me will never go hungry" (John 6:35). He was not going to provide them with manna. He provided himself.

And yet, when Jesus confronted the religious leaders about their unwillingness to believe, he focused on the miracles. "The miracles I do in my Father's name speak for me" (John 10:25 NIV). When they were ready to stone him for blasphemy, he told them, "I have shown you many great miracles from the Father. For which of these do you stone me?" (10:32 NIV). Commented John: "Even after Jesus had done all these miraculous signs in their presence, they still would not believe in him" (12:37 NIV).

How to make sense of this? Jesus, who tried to hush up his miracles, and who told the Pharisees they were wicked to demand them, also told them that the miracles they had witnessed demonstrated that he came from God.

The answer has to do with the nature of signs. As Professor Colin Brown writes, "When I drive along the freeway and see a green sign that reads 'Pasadena—Next Eleven Exits,' I am not being treated to a logical demonstration that each and all of the next eleven off ramps will lead me to Pasadena. I am being given a pointer. Only in following the directions of the sign do I discover whether the sign is telling the truth or not."[1]

Brown also writes, "Miracles are like warning flags. They signal the presence of a different order of reality that is present in the midst of our everyday world."

Signs are never an end in themselves. They do not point to themselves. They are not beautiful in themselves. They do not do the really important work by themselves. They exist to lead us somewhere, not to make us think we have arrived.

When I cross the Golden Gate Bridge and see highway signs for my hometown of Santa Rosa, I get a warm feeling. I am on my way home.

If I get lost and, after wandering helplessly up one street and down another, I happen on a sign that points me toward my destination, I am flooded with relief.

Yet in neither case do I stop to admire the sign. And when I arrive at my destination, I do not tell others about the sign. It is hardly worth mentioning. It only serves to point me on my way.

Jesus did miracles. They met human need, and they showed him for what he really was: God's own messenger. Anybody (like some Pharisees) who saw that and pretended not to get the message was a hypocrite. They might say they were looking for light, but in truth they didn't want to see it. They saw the highway sign and decided to take another route.

Jesus' calling was not to do miracles, but to proclaim the good news that the kingdom of God was breaking in—through him! Signs and wonders were a natural aspect of that eruption of heaven into earth. But the point wasn't signs and wonders. They were symptoms, not substance.

1. Colin Brown, *That You May Believe: Miracles and Faith Then and Now* (Grand Rapids, MI: Eerdmans, 1985), 107.

This is a crucial perspective for understanding the place of miracles in Jesus' day and in our own day. Any time we turn the focus on miracles rather than on what they signal, we get off track. They are signs, not destinations; symptoms, not substance. If we try to make substance out of them, we end up losing the focus God wants for us.

Some people act more interested in miracles than in Jesus. That approach will lead you in the wrong direction.

And yet . . . signs and wonders are a most natural symptom of heaven breaking in. If we, like those Pharisees, turn our backs on them, we put ourselves in serious spiritual danger.

We are responsible to be open for signs of God's wondrous presence, and to pray for them. We are responsible to praise God when we see miracles, and to think about what message God has for us in them.

We are equally responsible not to go pursuing signs and wonders as though they were the ultimate good that God intended. They are not the substance of the kingdom; they are symptoms of the kingdom. The substance is the presence of Jesus, who suffered, died, and was buried, then was raised again to life. Nothing, not even miracles, can substitute for him.

Two further questions arise. First, did the signs and wonders of Jesus' time mark a one-time eruption of God's power, like what happened in Moses' day? In that case, we shouldn't necessarily expect the same signs and wonders in our day.

Or had a door been opened that would never close? Did Jesus' signs and wonders represent a new regime that had broken in, never to leave?

Second, when Jesus sent out his disciples with the authority to do miracles, was that authority just for those mission trips, or did it establish a pattern for Jesus' disciples for all time?

Since the Reformation, most Protestant Christians have believed (along with Calvin and Luther) that miracles mainly stopped when the Bible was finalized. There might be exceptions during revivals or in foreign missions, but in general, miracles weren't necessary. The theory was that signs and wonders had done their job in Jesus' day, accrediting Jesus' gospel. But when the Bible was published, that accreditation was no longer needed. The Bible replaced miracles as the source of authority.

Pentecostalism came along proclaiming a different theory—that Christians had missed out on God's power for all those years. Miracles had largely disappeared because Christians lost sight of God's intentions for them. Pentecostals respected the Reformation as beginning a restoration of the true gospel and the true church. They believed that Pentecostalism would complete it, that signs and wonders would become normal again and would usher in the day of the Lord.

Shortly before his death, Jesus made a prediction about what his disciples would do after he left them. "Very truly I tell you, whoever believes in me will do the works I have been doing, and they will do even greater things than these, because I am going to the Father" (John 14:12).

Pentecostals often translate this to say that we are supposed to do even bigger miracles than Jesus did. Non-Pentecostals respond that Jesus can't mean miracles, since nobody has ever done miracles like he did. Peter and John and Paul healed many, but as far as we can tell, it was nothing like the number that Jesus did. And they never turned water into wine or walked on water.

Non-Pentecostals say Jesus must refer to other things—most likely the spread of the gospel across ethnic boundaries to billions of people around the world. Jesus never reached non-Jews in any number, and even among Jews, his real converts were few. The spectacular rise of the church in Acts and its continued growth through the centuries since is the "greater thing" that Jesus meant.

Even though I think the non-Pentecostals have the better argument, it shouldn't obscure the fact that Jesus' disciples continued to do miracles after his ascension, and that those miracles were extraordinarily important to the early growth of the church. In fact, if Jesus' "greater things" does refer to the spread of the gospel, it's worth noting how often extraordinary growth in numbers or breakthroughs into new cultures come closely linked to miracles. The two—growth and miracles—often walk closely. That was certainly true of the early church.

You do not have to read far into the book of Acts to know that miracles did not stop with Jesus. The first Christian church, beginning in Jerusalem and soon spreading through the Mediterranean region, experienced powerful miracles. They started immediately at Pentecost with the sights and sounds of the Holy Spirit's baptism—tongues of fire and the sounds of a mighty wind. Soon Peter healed a begging crippled man in just the way Jesus would have. Ananias and Sapphira died in a miracle of judgment. "The apostles performed many miraculous signs and wonders among the people" (Acts 5:12 NIV).

When serious persecution began and those early Christians scattered, the miracles did not stop. Philip did miracles in Samaria. Peter saw visions, and after being arrested, had an angel lead him out of prison. Later, Peter raised Dorcas from the dead. In two miracles of judgment, King Herod died suddenly and Elymas the sorcerer was struck blind.

When Paul, miraculously converted, began to travel with Barnabas, Acts 14:3 says that God "confirmed the message of his grace by enabling them to do miraculous signs and wonders" (NIV).

Paul and Barnabas went to Jerusalem to defend their ministry before a church council, and there they described "miraculous signs and wonders God had done among the Gentiles through them" (15:12 NIV). A vision led Paul to go into Greece, and in Philippi he exorcised an evil spirit from a young slave girl. The authorities threw him in prison with his companion Silas, and a miraculous earthquake released them. Paul went on to Thessalonica, Athens, Corinth, and Ephesus, where he settled down for two years. "God did extraordinary miracles through Paul, so that even handkerchiefs and aprons that had touched him were taken to the sick, and their illnesses were cured and the evil spirits left them" (Acts 19:11–12).

After that, no more miracles are described. As Acts progresses, signs and wonders seem to grow less frequent—or else Luke feels that he has established them so well that he doesn't need to keep mentioning them. Whichever is the case, nobody could read Acts without recognizing that miracles were as much a part of the early church's ministry as they were a part of Jesus' ministry.

Paul wrote to the Corinthians that they had seen in his ministry "the marks of a true apostle, including signs, wonders and miracles" (2 Corinthians 12:12). He wrote to the Romans about "what Christ has accomplished through me in leading the Gentiles to obey God by what I have said and done—by the power of signs and miracles, through the power of the Spirit" (Romans 15:18–19 NIV). Clearly for Paul, just as for Luke, gospel work continued to be accompanied by signs and wonders. There is no indication anywhere in the Bible that those miracles would stop, ever.[2]

Whether all believers did miracles is less clear. Paul wrote to the Corinthians listing miracles as one of the gifts of the Spirit. Some, he writes, have the gifts of healing, some miraculous powers, some prophecy, some tongues. Obviously these gifts were familiar to the church, but it doesn't seem that everybody had them—only some.

Paul's teaching to the churches in his various letters always emphasizes prayer, love, and faithful unity in the Spirit. He never tells Christians that he expects them to heal or cast out demons. (Nor does he tell them to launch evangelistic crusades.) Arguments from silence are unreliable. Just because he didn't tell them to do it doesn't prove he didn't want them to do it. It is striking, though, how different his priorities were from some who practice healing and exorcism today. They talk about doing miracles every chance they get. Paul didn't.

Miracles were integral to the spread of the gospel, not just in Jesus' ministry but for those who spread the word after him. However, for neither Jesus nor the apostles did signs and wonders become the centerpiece. Rather, they endorsed what Jesus and the apostles did. They were a normal and notable sign pointing to what God was about, but they were

---

2. Some people point out that the last paragraph in 1 Corinthians 13, the "love chapter," predicts an end to tongues and prophetic words of knowledge. It does, but Paul is clearly referring to Christ's return, when "perfection comes" (1 Corinthians 13:10) and we see God face-to-face.

not a focal point. Unquestionably important, they were not intended to take over our attention.

Surely the New Testament tells us two crucial facts about miracles: Christian ministry is marked by them, but Christian ministry doesn't focus on them. That's a delicate balance that many get wrong.

8

Did Miracles Happen After the Apostles?

Many people dislike history. Their eyes glaze over when they see references to ancient characters with strange names, especially people who wore robes and spoke Latin.

Because they avoid history, many Christians develop their philosophy of life using just two large chunks of reality: the Bible and their personal experience. On the subject of miracles, you find people operating as though, outside of the Bible, healing was first practiced last month at the "Desperate for Jesus" conference. (If they're old and gray, they may refer back as far as John Wimber, or even Oral Roberts. That covers about 3 percent of the time since Jesus.) It's as though no Christians lived in the centuries in between, or if they did, we can learn nothing from them.

If we pay no attention to history, we lose the wisdom and experience of other Christians. Jesus promised never to leave his followers but instead to be "with you always, to the very end of the age" (Matthew 28:20). The plain meaning is that you can find Jesus at work among his people at any point in history—even times when people had very different ideas than we do. They, too, are part of the body of Christ. Jesus was with them (and still is; we will meet them when heaven comes to earth).

History is valuable, but history can be hard. Most of it comes from documents that answer questions we weren't asking, using terminology we barely get.

And we wonder whether we should believe what we read in those documents, especially about miracles. Were people in those old times more gullible than we are? Did their lack of scientific knowledge make them credulous? Modern people naturally distrust old reports.

Consider this excerpt from a very ancient text, *The Martyrdom of Polycarp*:

> When [Polycarp] had . . . finished his prayer, those who were appointed for the purpose kindled the fire [to burn him to death]. And as the flame blazed forth in great fury, we to whom it was given to witness it beheld a great miracle and have been preserved that we might report to others what then took place. For the fire, shaping itself into the form of an arch, like the sail of a ship when filled with the wind, encompassed as by a circle the body of the martyr. And he appeared within, not like flesh which is burnt, but as bread that is baked, or as gold and silver glowing in a furnace. Moreover, we perceived such a sweet odor, as if frankincense or some such precious spices had been smoking there. At length, when those wicked men perceived that his body could not be consumed by the

fire, they commanded an executioner to go near and pierce him through with a dagger. And on his doing this, there came forth a dove and a great quantity of blood, so that the fire was extinguished, and all the people wondered that there should be such a difference between the unbelievers and the elect.[1]

Should we believe that? Flesh glowing like gold and silver? A dove appearing from the dying Polycarp's side?

Some people (including many historians) start out believing that miracles just don't happen. They would automatically consider this story a legend, with little or no truth value. Of course, they treat all miracles—including biblical miracles—that way.

Other people, like me, try to stay open-minded. Is there any philosophical or scientific reason to rule miracles out-of-bounds completely? I don't know of one.

Still, you have to ask questions, and the first and most important is the question of credible witnesses. You should only believe an extraordinary story like this if you have very good reasons to believe the witnesses. Are they sober eyewitnesses, known for their careful reporting? Do other witnesses corroborate their testimony? Do the reports have "the ring of truth"?

Such questions don't give you a formula for what to believe. You still have to make a personal assessment. Like a member of a jury listening to testimony in court, you must assess the credibility of the witnesses based on their character and background, based on other information you possess about the event, and ultimately based on whether the testimony sounds believable.

---

1. (*Martyrdom of Polycarp* 15–16 [A.D. 155])

I'll venture my opinion: I don't quite believe this version of Polycarp's martyrdom. I'm sure his death was moving and amazing, but the language of this account sounds too much like a legend, too little like a factual report. If not for the dove, I'd probably give it the benefit of the doubt, but that detail goes over the top. I'd need more than one witness to believe it.

I can't absolutely say it's exaggerated. I just say I'm skeptical. I'm not going to put any weight on it.

The same questions arise for biblical miracles, of course. And similarly, many historians are skeptical. They have every right to be. It's completely legitimate for historians to question the stories of miracles, just as they would such stories in any ancient document.

But the Bible's accounts of Jesus' miracles are different from the account of Polycarp's martyrdom. The language is different. The Gospels don't read like legends; they sound like factual accounts.

Plus, the stories come from multiple witnesses, not only in the four Gospel accounts, but in the unified belief of the eleven apostles (and many others) who gave their lives to serve Jesus based on the truthfulness of these stories. Nothing stands or falls on whether Polycarp's death was accompanied by miracles. He was a martyr with or without them. Jesus' miracles, though, are not "extra." They are intrinsic to the whole story of who Jesus was and how he introduced the kingdom of God.

Of all Jesus' miracles, the resurrection is best testified to, largely because his death was a public execution. All of Jerusalem was watching. The power structures had a vested interest in keeping Jesus dead, and given any way to debunk the claim that he had risen, they would surely have taken it. Instead, you find his disciples preaching about his resurrection at the town center in spite of threats meant to shut them up. Why would they do that if it weren't true? How would they do that if it were a simple matter to contradict their story? There is historical credibility to Jesus' resurrection—so long as you don't rule it out before you begin.

Conceivably you could believe one part of Jesus' story and not another—say, believe in the resurrection but not the feeding of the five thousand. But the force of the argument runs the other way. If the keystone of the story is true, that is reason to hope that all the parts of the story are true. It all wraps together.

Regarding Polycarp, it's not so. The miracles reported around his death mainly stand or fall by themselves.

In one sense, though, Polycarp's story *is* part of Jesus' story. Jesus said he would never leave his people. He told Peter he would build his church on a rock, a solid foundation. So the church all through history has a claim on Jesus. If Jesus was credible, then his people ought to be credible. That is, they ought to be credible in general, but there's no reason to think that Christians should always, and at all times, be credible.

Surely many of the miracle stories we hear *aren't* true. However, if we believe that Jesus really sent his Spirit to the church, we should listen with an open and hopeful mind to what Christians say at all times and places. If they report miracles, it's not irrational to pay attention. Such reports fit with the overall story. Jesus did miracles, his apostles did miracles—so why shouldn't his followers in later times do miracles, too?

That's exactly what you find when you check out the history. Miracles never stopped. At least, they never stopped being reported.

Some Christians have claimed that miracles ended when the Bible was put together as a book. As we'll see in a moment, they had their reasons for advancing that claim. The plain testimony, however, is that miracles continued.

In the first centuries after Jesus, many reputable Christian leaders wrote about miracles they knew of firsthand. Irenaeus reported on a man who was raised from the dead. Tertullian mentioned that the poison of scorpions' stings was neutralized when Christians responded in faith. Eusebius recorded an Easter vigil that ran out of oil for their lamps, until Narcissus prayed over water that turned into oil. Athanasius mentioned bishops who did miracles (as well as some who didn't). Basil, in describing the greatness of Gregory Thaumaturgus, said that he cast out demons, brought whole regions to Christ, made rivers change their courses through prayer, caused a lake to dry up, and had prophetic insight into the future.

Jerome described how Hilarion prayed over three sick children and healed them. John Chrysostom wrote of several judgment miracles in his day—a fire that stopped the reconstruction of the temple in Jerusalem, and death that overtook two men who made fun of the sacred temple vessels.

These aren't just odd names I've listed. They are some of the most famous and reputable Christian leaders of those first centuries after Jesus. It never crossed their minds that miracles had ceased.

Augustine, who published *The City of God* in 419, gives perhaps the most detailed firsthand account of miracles in his day. He is a particularly convincing witness, given his brilliant mind and outstanding education. His theological and philosophical writings remain hugely influential to this day.

Not only was he extraordinarily insightful, Augustine had practical experience. He became a Christian as an adult and went on to oversee a large number of pastors and churches. In his long life he experienced extraordinary events, not least of which was the fall of Rome to barbarians from the north. Responding to that civilizational crisis from his home in North Africa, Augustine wrote *The City of God*. As one brief part of that massive treatise, he wrote about miracles.

Augustine was certainly not obsessed with miracles, nor was he naïve. He knew that miracles were unlikely, and he was naturally skeptical, yet many years as a pastor convinced him that miracles really occurred.

Augustine begins with a common question: Why had miracles ceased?

> Why, they say, are those miracles, which you affirm were wrought formerly [in New Testament times], wrought no longer?

Earlier in his career, Augustine had himself believed that miracles had largely stopped with the apostles. Experience had changed his mind.

> Even now miracles are wrought in the name of Christ, whether by His sacraments or by the prayers or relics of His saints; but they are not so brilliant and conspicuous as to cause them to be published with such glory as accompanied the former [biblical] miracles. . . . These modern miracles are scarcely known even to the whole population in the midst of which they are wrought. . . . For frequently they are known only to a very few persons, while all the rest are ignorant of

them . . . and when they are reported to other persons in other localities, there is no sufficient authority to give them prompt and unwavering credence, although they are reported to the faithful by the faithful.[2]

In other words, miracles continue to happen, but they don't get publicized. There's no motive to publicize them, since they aren't tied directly to the Good News of Jesus. People in the same neighborhood don't hear of them, and people in far-off places have no particular reason to believe in whatever reports reach them.

When I set out to write this book, I would have said that times have changed. I would have said that any hint of a miracle gets reported and over-reported to the point of exaggeration. Televangelists and megachurch pastors publicize everything.

I've changed my mind. Yes, there is hype and over-reporting. But as I've asked ordinary people whether they have ever seen a miracle, I've heard many credible stories. None of them has been widely reported. In fact, sometimes the person's own family has never heard the story.

Dale Flowers, my pastor, told me of a mission trip he took to China with a group of pastors in 1993. They were being chauffeured in a minibus down a remote, narrow road clogged with trucks. Vehicles, including their own, were passing each other at every opportunity. It was dusk, raining, and tense driving conditions, when an oncoming truck loaded with logs attempted to pass. As the truck swerved into their lane, the load of logs shifted and lifted the truck off two of its wheels. To Dale and his fellow passengers, it

---

2. Saint Augustine, *The City of God*, trans. Marcus Dods, DD, Google Books.

appeared that only one of two things could happen: either the truck would tip over in their lane and they would crash into it, or the truck with its load of logs would fall on their minibus. They had nowhere to escape and no time to slow down. In an instant it became clear that they would all die. Dale didn't even have time to pray.

Then, defying the laws of gravity, the leaning truck was righted back on all four wheels and completed its pass without crashing into their vehicle. It was as if God had caught the falling truck, lifted it, and moved it out of the way of their minibus. Absolutely stunned by their escape, the pastors—ordinarily a talkative bunch—didn't say a word. Afterward, no one mentioned what had happened. And certainly, though I have heard Dale talk about the incident privately, I have never heard him preach of it in all his years of preaching.

You can understand why. The miracle made a difference to those pastors, but what difference would it make for others? If they weren't there to see it for themselves, they would probably be skeptical. Why press it?

That's the atmosphere Augustine describes in his day, too. He tells of a healing that he saw with his own eyes in Carthage. Innocentius had been treated for fistulas through a very painful surgery, but one fistula—a wound in the anal cavity—had remained. Innocentius was terrified of another operation—remember, there was no anesthetic and a great likelihood of deadly infection. His doctors assured him that medicine would heal the wound without surgery.

Days went by, however, and the fistula did not heal. Eventually the surgeons concluded that they would have to cut after all. Innocentius became hysterical. "There arose in the house such a wailing, in sympathy with the excessive despondency of the master, that it seemed to us like the mourning of a funeral," says Augustine, who was present.

The night before the operation, as his friends knelt to pray, Innocentius

> cast himself down, as if someone were hurling him violently to the earth. . . . With what earnestness and emotion, with what a flood of tears, with what groans and sobs, that shook his whole body, and almost prevented him speaking, who can describe? . . . I could not pray at all. This only I briefly said in my heart: "O Lord, what prayers of Thy people dost Thou hear if Thou hearest not these?"[3]

"The dreaded day dawned." Innocentius' Christian friends came to support him through the operation, as they had promised to do. The surgeons appeared with their frightful instruments. Innocentius was laid out, his bandages untied. The surgeon probed for the place to cut. He found, to his amazement, that the wound was completely healed.

Though a miraculous healing had occurred in plain daylight, Augustine makes the point that very few people have ever heard the story. He continues with other stories of healings that he knows firsthand. A woman is cured of breast cancer. A doctor is healed of gout. A man from Curubis, a town near Carthage, was cured of paralysis and of a hernia at the moment of his baptism, and he came to Augustine to give an account of what had happened.

Hesperius, suffering under the malice of evil spirits, asked for prayers, and his torment ceased. Another young man in the neighborhood was healed of paralysis.

3. Ibid.

In a place called Victoriana, a young man lay near death in a chapel, possessed by an evil spirit. When a young woman began to sing hymns, the man screamed and grabbed on to the altar. By prayer, the evil spirit was cast out, and the young man's eye, which had been badly injured, was dramatically healed.

For several pages, Augustine goes on describing miracles he has witnessed or knows of firsthand.

> What am I to do? I am so pressed by the promise of finishing this work, that I cannot record all the miracles I know; and doubtless several of our adherents, when they read what I have narrated, will regret that I have omitted so many which they, as well as I, certainly know. . . . Were I to record exclusively the miracles of healing which were wrought in the district of Calama and of Hippo by means of this martyr— I mean the most glorious Stephen—they would fill many volumes.[4]

He concludes, "Even now, therefore, many miracles are wrought, the same God who wrought those we read of [in the Bible] still performing them, by whom He will and as He will; but they are not as well known, nor are they beaten into the memory, like gravel, by frequent reading," as is the case with the Bible miracles. People hear about contemporary miracles but they forget, Augustine says, and they don't pass the stories on to others.

Nevertheless, Augustine says, miracles are real. He himself has witnessed them.

If you have never heard of Augustine's miracles, it is probably because the martyrs and their relics are so prominent in

---

4. Ibid.

these stories. They make Protestants intensely uncomfortable, and they make many modern Catholics uneasy, too.

In Augustine's time, though, they brought little suspicion. Martyrs had given the highest example of faith, since they had sacrificed their lives testifying to their belief in Jesus' resurrection. Though they were now with Jesus—or perhaps I should say *since* they were now with Jesus—people believed they could still play a part in what God did on earth. Exactly how that worked, Augustine said he didn't know. But he had seen for himself that miracles happened where the martyrs were buried. He obviously wasn't worried about it at the time.

Maybe he should have been. As centuries passed, the relics of the Christian martyrs grew even more prominent. Elaborate shrines grew up around their graves, and various body parts were distributed to churches across Europe. A toe might be in Nice, a finger in Frankfurt. People wanted to be buried near the relics of the saints in order to borrow a little of the saints' holiness in death. So the cemeteries around and in churches grew, and people's attention to life after death also grew, with speculations about purgatory and limbo and the ways in which the dead could be prayed for and to. By the late Middle Ages this had created a vast church machinery, with church leaders seemingly presiding over people's eternal destinies as they administered the church apparatus. This power over human destiny led to corruption—you could buy your way into heaven. As corruption rose, so ultimately did protests against corruption, leading to the Reformation.

Augustine never saw these problems coming. He knew from reading the Bible that a man was once raised from the dead by touching Elisha's bones (2 Kings 13:21). He knew that the apostle Paul had healed by sending a handkerchief he had touched (Acts 9:12). Might not the body of a martyr similarly convey some of his God-given authority? It didn't seem unreasonable or dangerous.

In retrospect we can see that miracles God did—"by whom He will and as He will," as Augustine put it—could get overshadowed by the means used to gain those miracles—which saints at which shrines using which prayers. Miracle-working procedures sometimes became the focus instead of the gospel of Jesus. The same thing can happen in our own time. Miracles are never as important as Jesus, and the way we pursue them should never overshadow our devotion to Christ.

Miracles gave tremendous prestige to the Catholic Church in the Middle Ages. Many, many miracles were recorded, sometimes in a form that seems almost modern in its historical detail. Bernard of Clairvaux, for example, healed hundreds of people as he traveled about Germany, and these healings are well documented, with times, places, and the names of witnesses recorded.

During the Reformation, when Martin Luther and John Calvin were leading the brand-new Protestant church, Roman Catholic authorities used these miracles to attack their credibility. "The Reformers have no miracles to back up their new teachings," these church leaders accused. What did that say about the authenticity of those teachings?

Surely miracles were God's stamp of approval. Surely they affirmed that the Catholics were God's true church.

It's not so far off from today, when some churches would make a similar challenge. If your teaching is so great, they ask, why don't you see miracles?

Calvin answered these accusations very directly. You can't establish the truth simply by pointing to miracles, he said, because not all miracles come from God. "We must remember that Satan has his miracles, too," Calvin wrote. (For example, Pharaoh's magicians did miracles [Exodus 7:11–12]; the slave girl in Acts 16:16 could predict the future by a spirit that possessed her; and Jesus warned in Matthew 7:22–23 that many people in the Last Judgment would protest that they did many miracles, only to be told by Jesus, "I never knew you!")

Miracles associated with relics and shrines, Calvin asserted, linked to a false gospel of superstition and human attempts to please God by our own efforts. They were false miracles accrediting a false gospel.

Furthermore, Calvin said, the Reformation churches *did* have accrediting miracles: Jesus' miracles and the apostles' miracles. Those were enough. They had accredited the true gospel of the Protestant churches—the gospel found in the Scriptures.

Calvin was pointing everyone's attention away from present-day signs and wonders and back to Jesus. A church could only be judged by its faithfulness to Jesus' gospel, which God had approved once and for all time, and clearly proclaimed in the Bible.

I believe Calvin was fundamentally right that miracles, in themselves, don't prove which church is genuinely faith-filled or Spirit-filled. That must be judged by the gospel the churches preach.

In those days it was mainly Protestants versus Catholics vying for approval, but today it is thousands of different, competing churches. Subtly or overtly they offer proofs of their righteousness: we have more miracles, we worship more enthusiastically, we pray more, we are friendlier, we do more for the poor, we teach the Bible better, etc. All these are important qualifications, but nothing can substitute for carrying Jesus' good news. The fundamental question for any church is: Are we faithful to Jesus and his gospel?

Christians are not the only ones to claim miracles. Hindu gurus, Muslim imams, and Buddhist shrines attract followers because of miracles, too. Only Christians tell of Jesus' saving death and resurrection.

Because miracles are spectacular, they seem to tell us all we need to know. But miracles don't tell anything unless they point toward Jesus. Follow me, Jesus said, the Way, the Truth, and the Life.

That still leaves an important question: Why didn't Calvin see miracles?

Calvin believed that miracles had stopped at the time of the apostles. He didn't get that from Scripture—there are no Bible verses that suggest such a thing. Calvin drew from experience. He had connections and friends in churches all over Europe. He evidently didn't know of anywhere that miracles occurred in what he considered a true gospel context.

There are two separate issues here. One is theological. Miracles never stopped being reported in the Catholic Church, nor among some Anabaptists. Calvin made a theological judgment that those miracles were illegitimate, because he believed the gospel those churches preached was illegitimate. Theologians are still arguing about that.

The second issue is purely observational. In the many places where Calvin believed a true gospel was preached, he knew of no miracles. He drew a general conclusion that miracles were now unnecessary. This set in motion a tradition that would last for the next three hundred years. Among most Lutherans, Methodists, Presbyterians, and Baptists—the vast majority of Protestants—miracles weren't part of the ordinary Christian life.

Exceptions cropped up on the mission field, during revivals, and among groups that had a particular emphasis on the Holy Spirit. John Wesley noted miracles in his diary. However, that wasn't the mainstream, even among John Wesley's followers.

I grew up in this mainstream heritage. My grandparents were missionaries to India, preaching the gospel of Jesus for all they were worth. My parents, too, were deeply faithful believers whose lives were dedicated to Jesus. However, I'd never heard of a miracle.

Why no miracles? One possibility is that mainstream Protestants lacked faith. Can that be so? Were they like the people in Jesus' hometown of Nazareth who had so little faith that even Jesus could do no miracles (Mark 6:5)?

While that was surely true of some, and possibly true of many, it's certainly not true of all. Many showed amazing faith, giving their lives in service to Jesus. They translated the Bible into hundreds of languages. They undertook world missions, giving their lives to spread the Good News.

Perhaps they just didn't ask God to do wondrous things. "You do not have because you do not ask," as James put it (James 4:2). I'm sure this was frequently true. If you believe miracles have stopped, and if you've never seen one, you don't regularly pray for them. However, I'm equally sure this didn't apply to everybody at every turn. When their children were sick, ordinary Christians in Calvin's churches surely begged God for his intervention. What could keep people who are suffering from asking God to heal? Surely they did ask, at least some of the time. But if miraculous healings took place, they didn't make an impression.

Only two other possibilities exist. Either Christians didn't recognize miracles when they happened because they weren't expecting them, or else God chose not to do miracles in those times and places.

Both seem possible. If miracles are rare and you aren't looking for them, you may not see them. I could wander through a diamond field and, if nobody told me to look for diamonds, I would probably never see one.

So with miracles. A church that has no awareness of the possibility that God wants to do miracles may never take note of what he does. They rarely ask, they never expect, and they aren't looking, so they don't see.

It's also possible that God just didn't do miracles. Remember that in the Old Testament, centuries sometimes passed without any record of signs and wonders. Jeremiah saw none. The Israelites who returned from Babylon saw none. And as we all know on an individual level, God doesn't always answer our personal prayers for miracles. Yet God is still at work. God is free to work in any way at any time, in the way that suits him. He doesn't have to do miracles at a certain, steady rate. He doesn't have to do them at all.

For many centuries, miracles were well attested, though sometimes in contexts that make us grimace. Then, for centuries, few if any miracles were reported in mainstream Protestant circles. And then finally, in the Pentecostal era, miracles came into the forefront again.

Surely we learn this from the history of miracles in the church: God freely accomplishes his purposes "by whom He will and as He will," as Augustine put it.

God was present and at work building his church in times of many miracles, no miracles, and "dubious" miracles, but "in all things God works for the good of those who love him" (Romans 8:28). It's a mistake to focus on miracles as the key to the kingdom. Life should be ordered in the other direction. "Seek first his kingdom and his righteousness, and all these things will be given to you as well" (Matthew 6:33).

9

The Pentecostal Revival of Miracles

However we understand miracles through the centuries—or the lack of them in some periods—we certainly live in a time of miracles today. The Pentecostal movement traces its beginnings to meetings in Los Angeles in 1906, the so-called Azusa Street Revival. An interracial, working-class revival erupted, patterned on the book of Acts. Speaking in tongues as a sign of the "baptism of the Holy Spirit" was the most dramatic development, but far from the only one. Those early Pentecostals expected to duplicate the life of the early church, miracles included.

From the very beginning, Pentecostalism created controversy. For the first fifty years it remained quite separate from other Christian churches, scorned and feared by mainstream pastors. Gradually, Pentecostalism became more acceptable, notably through the evangelist Oral Roberts. In the 1970s and 1980s, the charismatic movement brought its emphasis on the Holy Spirit into many mainstream denominations. Today if you wander randomly into a church service, you may find it difficult to tell whether you are with Pentecostals or Baptists—their preaching and worship can be quite similar.

Nevertheless, deep differences survive, as do deep feelings of difference. Pentecostals often believe that they are looked down on intellectually and theologically, and that hurts; non-Pentecostals sometimes feel that Pentecostals look down on them spiritually, and *that* hurts.

Regardless of feelings, every Christian has to contend with the powerful reality of Pentecostal faith. It has changed the shape of Christianity in virtually every denomination around the world. Pentecostals expect to see God work in tangible ways—to see miracle healings, to experience ecstasy and passion as they worship, to hear God speak audibly (or almost audibly), to witness many people turning away from sin and toward God, to see lives changed overnight. Pentecostals expect God to do great things, and (consequently?) they *see* God do great things. It's powerfully attractive to anyone who feels the pull of faith.

If you want to think seriously about miracles, you must take Pentecostalism into account. Wherever you go today, the two are linked.

Rather than try to describe the huge and highly varied Pentecostal scene, I'm going to use my life as a microscope. I am not Pentecostal or charismatic, but I have had opportunities galore to witness the Pentecostal and charismatic movements—not only in the United States, but all over the world. I want to spotlight a few moments in my experience with the hope that it represents a bigger slice of reality than just me. Then I want to consider how miracles fit in.

From the time I first encountered Pentecostals, I was drawn to them. At the same time I felt anxious because Pentecostals left me feeling second rate. Also, their claims didn't always fit my understanding of reality.

I've attended many services. I've met and talked at length with some outstanding leaders. I've thought long and hard about Pentecostal strengths and weaknesses. Let me say from the beginning that I love the Pentecostal and charismatic movements, and I'm grateful for how they have affected my life and the body of Christ worldwide.

I was raised in a different kind of Christianity, one that expresses deep feelings, deep prayer, and deep worship but only in a thoughtful, restrained manner. Uncontrolled emotion and hasty judgments scared us.

My upbringing reflected a deep love for the God who created the mind and spoke to the mind. C. S. Lewis would be our patron saint, if we believed in patron saints. Scripture was revered and *studied*. Doctrine was honored for illuminating the puzzles of life and Scripture. We loved hymns not so much for their beautiful words or music as for their tuneful crystallizations of biblical truth. I grew up in a passionate faith, but it was passion held close by the mind. Without the mind, passion was not trusted at all.

I realize that one can find all these same qualities within Pentecostalism, though they are not the movement's strengths. I also realize that others raised in my environment sometimes found it dry, legalistic, and joyless. But I never felt that way.

While I appreciated what I had grown up with, I longed for more. I think now that every Christian longs for more.

"Who hopes for what he already has?" as the apostle Paul put it (Romans 8:24). All I knew then, however, was that I craved a deeper intimacy with God and a deeper assurance that God was real and not my imaginary friend. Hearing my longing, God welcomed me to the charismatic movement.

I had some experience with charismatics in college, but nothing like what came immediately after I graduated when I took a job at a small company that published charismatic books and magazines. I wasn't worried about being involved with a charismatic group. Actually, I looked forward to it, if a little nervously.

I did have worries about my boss, whom I'll call Ray, a corpulent and very pushy individual. Ray was a big talker. Right from day one he announced to me that he planned to someday make me editor in chief. He gave me the great privilege of ghostwriting missionary Bruce Olson's biography, *Bruchko,* which is still in print.

Who doesn't want to come straight out of college and have the boss love you? What writer doesn't want such opportunities to publish? All the same, Ray made me nervous. I wasn't sure about him and his big talk.

The company was a great place to start out. Because it didn't have established procedures and it ran on a shoestring, you got to try anything and everything. (I got paid $100 a week, which even then was scandalously low, but I didn't care—I just wanted to be in publishing.) I met some wonderful people there and learned my way around the basics of the industry. Everything was great—or almost everything.

Ray wanted me to speak in tongues, and he wasn't subtle about it. In principle that was all right with me—I wanted to speak in tongues, too. I had asked God many times to show himself in unmistakable ways, and people told me that tongues could settle such doubts. The trouble was, though I asked God for tongues, nothing happened. No language came. People prayed for me with no result.

Ray announced that he was laboring in prayer for me. He wanted me to let go, to stop holding back. (Was I holding back? I didn't mean to.)

I never did gain the gift of tongues. I gained a measure of wisdom. Being surrounded daily by people who celebrated the Spirit, who testified to dramatic Pentecostal change in their lives, I came to understand charismatic testimonies in context. I was young and inexperienced in the world, but I gradually realized that they no more had life figured out than I did. Something powerful and wonderful had happened to them, but life still retained the old familiar anxieties and tangles. They weren't perfect, and they weren't settled. This was a valuable lesson. With all respect, a person's life is more than the sum of his religious experiences. I learned that you can't have anybody else's relationship with God; you can only have yours. I began the long process of learning to be comfortable with who I was and the way God has chosen to love me.

I learned how to listen to people's stories in a way that's trusting and hopeful, but also watchful. Whatever people say, life is never black and white; there are various shades of gray. The Bible wonderfully reflects that. Its people truly struggle with God and are blessed by God, but they retain all their ordinary human qualities, good and bad. Can you name one biblical character, other than Jesus, who doesn't have obvious faults? That's how real people are, whether they have experienced the baptism of the Holy Spirit or not.

Also, I didn't see any miracles. I heard people talk about them. I was quite willing to believe that they experienced them. But in the day-in, day-out workaday world, miracles didn't show up any more than they did in a Presbyterian publishing house. Life in a charismatic publishing house is pretty ordinary. You edit and sell books.

I think it was there that I began to suspect that miracles are rare. Rare, even in places where people sometimes talk as though they can be turned on like tap water.

After about six months, I got an unexpected job offer from *Campus Life* magazine, a publication just around the corner. *Campus Life* was a much higher-quality magazine than the publication I was working at and, after considerable thought and prayer, I took the job and announced to Ray I was leaving.

He tried everything he could to get me to stay—promises, fulsome praise, insulting imprecations. I particularly remember his saying that God had told him and his wife, after hours on their knees in prayer, that I was not to leave. It was a clear word from the Lord.

I told him that God would have to tell me the same thing.

"But have you really prayed?" he wanted to know. "Have you spent *hours* on your knees?" I had to admit I had not. But I had prayed, and that would have to be good enough.

At *Campus Life* I was a lot more comfortable. I worked with a mix of charismatic and non-charismatic Christians, joined together by the focus on reaching young people. It was a wonderful place to work, but I never stopped feeling grateful for my first job and the good, caring people I met. Even Ray. I deeply appreciated their personal, passionate love for God, and their expectation that he could and would meet our needs—and more than meet our needs. That's the most basic strength of the charismatic and Pentecostal movements, as I see it: people expect so much from God in an unguarded, passionate way. He answers those prayers.

I have a tendency to play it safe with life and with God. Pentecostals and charismatics encouraged my longing, urging me to hope. I think they do that for the entire worldwide church.

———

Six years later I got another up-close exposure to Pentecostalism, this time lasting four years. Newly married, my wife Popie and I went to Kenya as missionaries with Youth for Christ. We had an extraordinary time there. I helped to start a magazine, hiring and training its staff; Popie taught classes in counseling. We became good friends with a number of Kenyan families, some of whom remain close to us today.

Friends our age or younger were nearly all caught up in a Pentecostal revival, and through them we got a front-row seat to the movement.

The Kenya Pentecostal revival began as a youth movement, primarily through high school and college fellowships. Almost every serious young Christian seemed to be infected. It was fresh and exciting, and no doctrinal battle lines had been drawn. I never heard anybody denigrate the faith of those (mostly their elders) who lacked the Pentecostal experience. Our friends seemed eager for anyone to catch the Spirit. They were ready to share, but not (in my experience) pushy or overbearing, and I never felt my own faith treated as second class. I only felt that wonderful, life-changing experiences were happening all around me.

Sometimes I got pushed out of my comfort zone. I remember attending one church service where, mysteriously, young men got up midservice and began pulling the shutters closed on all the windows. What was going on? In the darkened room we soon found out: There was shouting so loud we could hardly think, while the worshipers danced and jumped around the building. The shutters were closed to protect the neighbors.

I think it was during that same weekend—a trip to a rural boarding school—we awakened in the middle of the night to hear our hosts praying loudly. This was a wonder to us. We had never been around people who woke up in the night and prayed at the top of their voices for hours.

We didn't attend the all-night prayer meetings that our younger friends often participated in—sleep was too precious to us—but we heard about them. We heard all kinds of stories of power encounters, of miracles, and of prophecies. I heard of a river that miraculously dried up, allowing a stranded family to cross over. I heard of money miraculously provided. I heard of a young woman, tormented by demons, healed instantaneously when people prayed.

I never *saw* a miracle in Kenya—but I don't doubt they happen, and that in some times and places many happen.

I did see many young people become Christians with a vigorous, active faith. They were eager to go anywhere and do anything to share with others. Nowadays when I return to Kenya, I see that their early innocence has sometimes turned sour, especially where the Prosperity Gospel has taken hold and a shallow, materialistic message tickles people's ears.

Nevertheless, I can't forget the excitement of those early years. They left a very positive idea of faith exercising itself in hope. The focus was on God and the gospel. Anything seemed possible with God. That God-centered optimism and activism are hallmarks of Pentecostalism, and a gift to the entire church.

My third phase of interaction with Pentecostalism has come through decades of work as a writer and reporter for *Christianity Today* magazine. In that capacity I have observed and interviewed many Pentecostals and charismatics as part of the worldwide church. It covers a great deal of variety: in the U.S. and overseas, with famous leaders as well as grassroots Christians, and among people of many different ethnicities.

Rather than try to sum up all I've seen, let me focus on two leaders. One was John Wimber, who led a large Southern Californian church called The Vineyard. In the 1980s, Wimber was very well-known internationally as a speaker and an author. He presented the charismatic movement in a style that appealed to educated, middle-class people. He also helped teach a course in miracle-working at Fuller Theological Seminary in Pasadena, which included a "practicum" where students were taught how to pray for signs and wonders to occur. This would not have caused a stir at a Pentecostal school, but at Fuller, founded by conservative evangelicals, it created an uproar.

When I first met him, Wimber had recently published a book, *Power Evangelism,* which suggested that miracles

happen all the time. God spoke to Wimber, telling him intimate details about strangers he had just met. Wimber saw
messages imprinted on people's foreheads and experienced
dramatic congregational meltdowns—trembling and fits—
when the Spirit began to work. Many people were healed of
incurable diseases. Wimber was clearly fascinated with the
possibility of raising people from the dead, and he eagerly
expected to see that, too.

Having read his books and listened to recordings of his
talks, I expected somebody aggressive and outspoken. I found
a teddy bear. Wimber wore loose-fitting shirts and struggled
with his weight. He had a very relaxed, Southern California
style and a welcoming personality. I liked him immediately,
and I felt he liked me.

Several memories of our lengthy conversations stand
out. At one point I asked Wimber what changes he wanted
American churches to make. He answered that he was not
trying to fundamentally change American churches; he just
wanted them to pray for the sick.

"I can't imagine a church that doesn't pray for the sick"
was my immediate, startled response.

We went back and forth a few times before we could figure
out what the other was saying. Wimber meant public prayer
for healing, with the whole congregation actively aware and
participating. I meant prayer of a quieter kind.

Christians pray. The debate between charismatics and non-
charismatics is not over whether to pray. The debate is over
how to pray: with what exuberance, with what publicity,
with what expectation, and sometimes with what words. I
think both sides have something to offer. There's a place for
quiet prayers. Those, after all, were the prayers that Jesus

endorsed in Matthew 6:5–8, when he warned his disciples not to imitate those who make big, public prayers. He taught his followers to pray privately and briefly.

Even so, I think charismatics did the whole church a favor by taking prayers for healing out of the closet. I think it helps to offer very public opportunities for people in need to come ask for prayer. Doing so has undoubtedly led to more prayers for healing, and more expectation and hope for signs and wonders to occur. (My own Presbyterian church now invites people to the front after services for prayer, and I know we are far from the only ones. That would never have happened in the church I grew up in.)

When I visited Wimber's church, I appreciated the non-pressuring style. They didn't turn healing prayers into a spectacle. They were warm. They were kind. I didn't detect any sense of shame or blame for those whose prayers weren't answered. The time of prayer after every service clearly conveyed a message: As a church, we are asking God for help, and we expect to see him work. We are *excited* to see him work.

It's good for a church to make that statement publicly.

Another aspect of my conversation with Wimber troubled me somewhat. I asked if I could talk to people who had been healed at The Vineyard. From reading Wimber's books and hearing him speak, I would have thought he could have chosen from a long list of regular members, but apparently not. Wimber and his staff kicked it around for a while. They didn't really keep records, they said. What had happened to that guy who had his heart disease miraculously healed? They didn't remember where he had gone, and they certainly didn't have an up-to-date address. In the end, they weren't any help to me in finding the healed and the helped.

I accept that they were a big church with a lot of visitors coming and going. But if miracles are happening frequently in a church, you ought to be able to put your hand on a few people who can tell a visitor about it. The quality of their testimony wasn't as good as I had hoped. They certainly wouldn't have impressed a skeptic.

I'm sure wonderful things had happened—but maybe not quite as many as I had thought. I suspect they heard stories and took them at face value, passing them along. I think that happens a lot where miracles are concerned. It doesn't do anything for credibility.

When I ended my first John Wimber interview, I asked him to pray for me. He was taken aback, and maybe a little suspicious that I was trying some kind of journalistic trick. I wasn't. I knew that whatever critique I might make of him, I wanted some of what he had.

"What do you want me to ask God for?" he asked.

I shook my head. "I don't have anything particular in mind. I want whatever God wants for me. I want to be blessed."

He put his hands on me as I bowed. "Is something bothering you in your stomach?" he asked. Wimber was famous for getting words from God revealing people's troubles.

"No, nothing," I said.

"You're worried about your wife?"

"No, not particularly."

He hadn't discerned my needs, but he prayed for me. I think it's the proper way to relate, whether charismatic or Pentecostal or Presbyterian or Baptist. We pray for each other. I am grateful that John Wimber prayed for me. He is gone now—I interviewed him again when his health was failing, not too long before he died—but he leaves a very positive memory.

The second leader who impressed me was Jack Hayford, a Pentecostal pastor who has been a leader in the Foursquare Church for many decades. A tall, thin man with a long Pentecostal heritage and an old-fashioned style, Hayford is very different from Wimber. Wimber became a believer as an adult, having been a rock musician. Hayford is a hymn composer. He grew up in the church and is straight as an arrow.

I sat through an intimate weeklong pastors' training conference with Hayford—a conference that he led almost single-handedly, speaking spontaneously throughout the day. His sincerity was very attractive. There seemed to be no show or pretense in the man: he said exactly what he believed, without nuance. And what he believed was passionately attuned to Jesus. When Hayford sang "All for Jesus," you had the sense that he meant it, body and soul.

He told a story, set early in his ministry, when he was a struggling pastor of a tiny church. Just down the block was Van Nuys Baptist, a booming megachurch that had received national attention. One day Hayford pulled up to a traffic light on the Van Nuys Baptist corner.

Hayford felt a burning sensation on his face, as though the building were on fire. Through an inner voice God spoke to him, reprovingly: "You could at least begin by looking at the building."

He turned and saw nothing but a modern brick structure. "What now?" Hayford asked.

"I want you to pray for that church," God said. "What I am doing there is so great, there is no way the pastoral staff can keep up with it. Pray for them."

As Hayford began to pray, he felt an overflow of love for Van Nuys Baptist. It seemed to take no effort. Through the days to come, the same sensation came to him every time he passed by a church—any church. "I felt an overwhelming love for the church of Jesus Christ. I realized I had them in pigeonholes."

A few days later he approached a large Catholic church. Having been raised to take strong exception to Catholic doctrine, he wondered whether he would have the same loving feelings. He did, and he heard another message from God: "Why would I not be happy with a place where every morning the testimony of the blood of my Son is raised from the altar?"

"I didn't hear God say that the Catholics are right about everything," Hayford said, remembering the experience that changed his ministry. "For that matter, I didn't hear him saying the Baptists are right about everything, nor the Foursquare." The message was simply that people at those churches cared about God. These were sites dedicated to Jesus' name. And he, Hayford, was supposed to love and pray for them.

I wish all church leaders had that rock-bottom sense of belonging to all God's people.

Both Wimber and Hayford built large and influential churches that prayed for miracles. They both would consider miracles to be a normal expectation in church life. Miracles were important to their ministries.

I'll remember them for other achievements, though: for building churches that have integrity and depth as they reach out and love their neighbors; for open-handed love toward those with different perspectives; for integrity and humility.

And that's as it should be. What did the apostle Paul want to be remembered for? What about Peter? James? What did Jesus want to be remembered for? They all did miracles, and miracles were important to their ministries, but miracles were never at the center of their work.

10

Global Pentecostalism

Internationally, Pentecostalism can be quite different from what we know in America. It's many, many times bigger, for one thing. It's extremely vital. Most of the Protestant Christians in the majority world[1] are Pentecostal or charismatic in practice, if not by denomination. Unlike North America and Europe, the church is growing, often at a rapid pace. Whether in China, Africa, India, or Brazil, believers clearly expect miracles and tell stories about miracles.

Those who haven't traveled much in these countries sometimes get the idea that miracles happen all the time, that it's fireworks every night and every place. We hear stories of amazing signs and wonders, and it seems that they are everyday events. Reality is more complex. In China, for example, the church has exploded, and miracle stories in many churches

1. "Majority world" denotes the non-Western, less-developed nations of the world that make up the majority of the world's population. The "global South," the "developing world," and the "Third World" are roughly synonymous.

are common. At the same time, China remains one of the most irreligious countries in the world, and most educated Chinese scoff at miracle stories. In this huge country, you may experience miracles if you belong to the right church, but the vast majority of people know nothing about them.

I was reminded of this complexity during a recent two-week trip to India. I visited four different locations around the country, and over two weeks I interviewed Indian Christians nonstop. Clearly, though they came from many denominations, most of them had a Pentecostal or charismatic orientation. I did not particularly ask about miracles, but as they described their lives and how they had come to trust in Jesus Christ, healings, exorcisms, and prophetic dreams got frequent mention. Miracles seemed to be the normal entry point for people becoming followers of Jesus. A few examples:

Chandra Lekha was given a Bible as a sixteen-year-old Hindu girl, but she didn't open it. She argued with Christians, "Why should we have a Western God?" She was determined to do well in school, especially as her tenth-grade exams approached that would decide whether she could go on for more education. Just before the exam, though, an epidemic of chicken pox hit the area. "There were deaths in every home." She came down with an especially serious case, covering her body with sores. Despite the fact that her whole family prayed, her sickness continued for more than two weeks.

"Then I remembered the Bible, the black book. 'If this black book says God is real, then God, why can't you stop the exam and heal me?' I prayed.

"The next morning I was completely dried up. Fear came over me. I began to read the book. Three days later I went to school, did the big exam, and passed with honors. I knew then that the Bible God was the true God."

For the first five years of her marriage, Bimba was barren. She miscarried three times. Bimba went to doctors and she did religious ceremonies and rituals, but nothing helped. Her husband, Ashok, got sick; his heart ached. A doctor examined him and gave a series of injections, but to no avail. "Both our lives were sadness," Bimba remembered.

Then a Christian neighbor visited their home and invited them to church. Bimba began to attend on Fridays and Sundays. People at church regularly asked how they could pray for her. A few months after their prayers began, she learned she was pregnant. Nine months later, she gave birth to a child.

Ashok resisted. He didn't want to go to church. Finally Bimba convinced him to try it. Once inside the church, he started to cry, then to shout. He lost control of himself until the pastor came and prayed. An evil spirit left him, and the pain he had been suffering went away. "I realized that this God is the one true God because no one else could help me."

Shivamma lives in a pipe—a large, concrete sewage pipe that was discarded by a nearby factory where she works. Her husband and two children live there with her. A local pastor discovered a squatter's village of people living in the pipes and began to try to help them with medical care and school for their children. "The pastor came to my home for prayer," Shivamma told me. "I didn't know why, or to whom he prayed. I thought Jesus was simply one of the gods."

Her daughter was terribly sick at three months of age. She was jaundiced and had passed blood. At the pastor's prayer, she was healed. "I realized this was the living God," Shivamma says.

The healing brought a wider impact. "We used to drink. Every day we would fight, fight, fight. Jesus Christ brought peace in our family. There's no fear because I trust him."

Near the end of my trip, I mentioned to an Indian medical doctor, Raju Abraham, that miracles seemed to be the predominant way for Indian people to come to faith. He politely disagreed. "No, Indians become Christians in all different ways. Some from reading the Bible, some from the witness of friends, some from attending a service and hearing someone make an appeal." And he added, "Earlier in my life, I tried to carefully determine what was a 'real' miracle and what was not. But eventually I realized that God is involved in every healing. People in the village attribute every healing to God, and they're right to do that. Whether it should be called a miracle is another matter."

After that conversation I went back to my notes. Looking at each person whose testimony I had recorded, I counted how many had mentioned miracles as part of the process of bringing them to God. I found Raju was right: the majority had not. Other entry points had led them to Christ. But the miracles stuck in my mind.

I think most people do as I had done. We notice the miraculous, overlooking the more "normal" ways people interact with God. It's a natural tendency.

In some situations, miracles *are* an unmistakable part of the story of a growing church. Clusters of miracles are often reported

- where people are illiterate and can't read the Bible. Miracles communicate the power of God in all languages;
- in polytheistic or animistic cultures that lack a mental framework to understand sin, guilt, and redemption. Miracles demand attention even if you don't yet grasp the nature of your problem and God's redemption;
- where no medical care can be had. Miracles represent the only hope for suffering people;
- where the spirit world is very real to people, including evil spirits—and a conflict of spiritual powers is out in the open. Miracles demonstrate power.

It's dangerous to generalize, as though God were obliged to follow our formula for where he should act. But certainly, some places see more miracles than others, and in some situations, miracles may be the only way to break through.

Just before completing this book, I was sent on a fact-gathering trip to Pemba, Mozambique, headquarters of Heidi and Rolland Baker and their organization, Iris Ministries. The Bakers are Pentecostal missionaries who came to Mozambique in 1995. After a brutal twenty-year civil war, Mozambique was among the poorest countries on earth.

Committed to serving the poor, the Bakers took on orphans and street children in Maputo, the capital. Their ministry has grown with astonishing speed. Now they lead a movement of over ten thousand churches, with thousands of abandoned children in their care and large programs of food distribution and economic development.

What gets the most attention for the Bakers, though, are miracles. They tell many amazing stories. Scores of Mozambican pastors claim to have raised people from the dead through prayer. Food has miraculously multiplied, blind people have had their sight restored, and the deaf and mute have regained hearing and speech. Heidi says, in fact, that in the region around Pemba, where they are now headquartered, God always gives a sign gift when they go on an outreach mission. One hundred percent of deaf people get their hearing restored through prayer, Heidi claims. Such miracles have accompanied a tremendous spread of the gospel in a nominally Islamic region that had few churches or missionaries when Iris first began to minister there.

Pemba is not an easy place to reach. From my home in California, I needed more than thirty hours of air travel to reach the tiny Pemba airport. Twenty-four hours later I was in a dinky six-seater airplane, on my way even farther out, to a rural outreach with Heidi and Rolland.

Circling out over the deep blue Indian Ocean and heading west, we transected miles of unmarked scrub with only occasional clusters of thatched-roof houses or a strip of dusty road to break the emptiness. We circled over a little-used dirt strip at a dry, brown place called Chiure. Before missionary pilot Joe Vaine hit the runway, we could see people running in our direction.

The crowd quickly swelled to several hundred. After landing and opening the tiny plane's door, Heidi waded into the sea of people while Rolland took photos.

Rolland says Heidi is fundamentally an introvert, longing for hours alone in prayer and meditation. Most of her days, however, are spent interacting one-on-one—with dirty and ragged children like these crowded around her, with their subsistence-farming mothers and fathers, with fellow Iris missionaries, with the students who joined us from Pemba by truck, and literally with anyone she encounters, high or low. One of the mottos she preaches is, "Stop for the one." She lives by it. As a result, she is prone to arriving late everywhere.

Rolland, who is in his sixties, grew up an Assemblies of God mission kid. Heidi is twelve years younger, a Laguna Beach teenage convert to Pentecostalism who heard God calling her to global missions. Shortly after their wedding, they left for Indonesia with a one-way ticket and little money. They have been missionaries ever since.

In Chiure we are far from civilization: no electricity, no running water. The only permanent building is a school with neither desks nor benches. The ground is flat and dry, waiting for the rainy season when crops can be planted by hand. I see no sign of tractors or even plow animals.

Chiure certainly fits the profile of a place to see miracles. Few people can read. Little or no medical care is available. Witchcraft is common.

The sun goes down fast at five thirty. On a screen mounted on one of the trucks, the *Jesus* film is shown. A crowd gathers on the open ground—Chiure offers no other entertainment—and grows to several hundred. Rapid-fire preaching begins after the film. After forty-five minutes of that, Heidi takes the microphone. First she leads a skit of the Good Samaritan. Then she announces that God is going to heal tonight, and invites anyone who is deaf to come forward.

I watch carefully, eager to see a miracle. "It always takes time [for the deaf to come]," Heidi later explained to me, "because if they are deaf, they can't hear your invitation. Someone has to go and get them."

Eventually four people come to the front. It is hard to see what happens next, for there is no stage, and the standing audience crowds forward. The only light comes from a blinding floodlight on the truck. Most of what happens is described over the booming sound system in Portuguese, translated into Makhuwa, the local language, with occasional English explanations for the approximately fifteen Westerners present.

Attention focuses on Antonio, a somber boy of perhaps twelve who, it is said, lost his hearing completely as a young child.

Of course Antonio cannot explain himself because he cannot hear, nor apparently can he speak. Heidi asks the audience for help. Do they know Antonio? Is he really deaf? Responses seem to come from only a few people, but Heidi is satisfied and proceeds to lay her hands on Antonio and pray.

Then she gives Antonio a microphone. "Ba-ba!" she shouts, the sound system amplifying her voice so loud as to make the deaf hear. "Ba-ba," Antonio repeats in a strangled, calf-like mew. "Ma-ma!" Heidi shouts. "Ma-ma," Antonio repeats. "Jesus," Heidi cues. "Jesus," Antonio answers.

Heidi announces jubilantly that Antonio is completely healed, and that, in fact, all four with hearing losses have been healed. She invites the crowd to praise God, but the response is weak. Later I ask her about this surprisingly subdued reaction. "It's always that way in Mozambique," she says. "They never show much reaction."

Her assistant, Antoinette, who has seen many Mozambican healings, agrees. "It seems odd," she says. "We would be jumping around."

After the deaf are healed, Heidi asks for those with bad backs to raise their hands so that members of the outreach team can find them and pray for them. Then come stomach problems. Finally, drunkards who want healing prayer are invited to identify themselves, and a few do. The evening program concludes with outreach team members circulating through the crowd, laying on hands and praying for anyone who indicates a desire for prayer. Plenty of people seem eager. Some of them indicate, through hand signals, that the prayers have made a difference.

It is during this period, Heidi later tells me, that the village chief approached her. "Did you see Antonio healed?" she asked him. He said he had seen it, and that the elders would like to donate land where Heidi could build a church doubling as a preschool and meeting center. They would also like Arco-Iris—the Portuguese name for Heidi and Rolland's organization, meaning "rainbow"—to come and drill a well. In Chiure, as in so many places in Mozambique, a healing miracle has opened the door to the gospel.

But was it truly a miracle? Unless you knew Antonio before and after, you couldn't say for sure that he was changed. Somebody with very poor hearing could have heard "Baba" and "Mama" roared out at that volume. Lacking local languages, it wasn't possible for me to press the point with the villagers, or with Antonio. (He spent the rest of the evening in his own world, not interacting.) I will always wonder whether I witnessed "a sign and a wonder" that night or not.

Nobody else seemed to wonder. We proceeded to a tent city set up by the approximately thirty students who have come by truck for this outreach. They are a mix of idealistic,

English-speaking Westerners in Pemba for a three-month "Harvest School," a kind of Pentecostal boot camp, and Mozambican Bible school students doing a different three-month course, training to be pastors. Heidi asks everyone she meets whether they witnessed Antonio's healing, and they all say they did.

After a night sleeping on the ground, the outreach team breakfasts with the chief and two other local elders, presenting them with gifts and honoring them through introductions and short speeches. Then the team splits up to go house to house, visiting and praying for people. Each group includes Mozambicans who can communicate in Portuguese if not in Makhuwa. Heidi says that this is where their ministry focus truly lies. The evening event merely introduces them for more personal interaction.

I follow Heidi and Rolland through the village with the three elders, discussing locations where the church and preschool could be built. At one point I see a man approaching from behind, wearing a white kaftan and *taqiyah* (Muslim cap). The area is Islamic and, as I watch him come up, I wonder what reaction he will bring. But he smiles and shakes hands all around, says he has heard that Issa [the Koran's name for Jesus] healed Antonio last night, and accepts the gift of a New Testament.

After saying good-bye to the elders with a prayer and a song, Heidi visits in homes. They are simple adobe structures of one or two rooms, their roofs made of a loose thatch, their floors dirt. Heidi has a gift for making friends—sitting with women by their front door, praying for them or their children, laughing and interacting. She seems completely at home, unintimidated by the poverty or the language barrier.

She prays for a boy with epilepsy. Though perhaps eight years old, he has not been in school. From the quarter-size scar on the top of his head, it looks as though he has been trepanned by a local medicine man. "Don't go back to the witch doctors," Heidi sings out as we move on.

At another home, Heidi sits with a smiling mother and her newborn, taking a language lesson in the local dialect. (She often makes friends this way, and perhaps because of it, speaks seven languages.) The mother says she must walk fifteen kilometers for water in this dry landscape. "This is why we drill wells," Heidi says to me. "Love looks like something."

For Heidi and Rolland, love looks like many things. They start schools, offer medical clinics, distribute food, drill wells. They also pray for miracles. All these forms of compassion open the way for the gospel. All of them are signs of God's love for those in need.

I spent a week in Pemba, a place thoroughly saturated with a belief in miracles. Many of the missionaries who work with the Bakers signed up after seeing healings that astonished them. Some of those miracles came through Heidi's bold prayer, but by no means all. "It's not just Heidi," Mozambican pastor Jose Lino told me. "I see the same miracles when I pray for healing. It doesn't happen because of our valiant efforts. It comes from God alone."

Pastors who train at their Bible school learn to pray for healing, and by all accounts the visible power of God leads to new Christians and new churches all over Mozambique. Often entire villages declare their allegiance to Jesus because they have seen people healed in his name. It's hard to remain skeptical when you hear so many such testimonies.

"When I was in Brazil," a young man named Egas Ngove told me, "many people asked, 'Why do miracles happen there and not here?' I said, 'Because people need them. They are desperate.'"

Added Pascual Mafuieque, "Mozambicans don't have many options in life. We don't have money [to go to the doctor]."

An Irish pastor who brings teams of young people to Pemba told me, "Here, healings come easily. We've prayed for the blind all over the world, and only five times have people been healed. But here, it happens most of the time. They pray for people and they get healed. To tell you the truth, I don't understand it."

Indiana University Professor Candy Brown was so intrigued by the Bakers' stories of healing that she attempted to verify them scientifically. With a small team, she traveled to Mozambique with audio and visual testing equipment. They accompanied Heidi on outreaches. Testing twenty-four Mozambicans before and after healing prayer—half by Heidi—the team detected statistically significant improvements in hearing and vision. (The results were published in the *Southern Medical Journal*, September 2010, and are available online.) Brown's team found similar results on an excursion to Brazil, but trials before and after prayer at charismatic conferences in North America did not yield significant results.

Even such scientific research can be doubted, though. When you read Brown's detailed report, you find that the testing was conducted under very difficult circumstances.

They were in the open air, with loud noises in the background, and often the people being tested didn't understand directions. Pressing buttons on the audiometer—a seemingly simple task—was quite beyond some of those being prayed for. Sometimes results had to be thrown out because the testing was too irregular. By scientific standards, twenty-four is a small sample size, and with these testing irregularities, it would be easy to cast doubt on the result.

Scientists would want to see whether someone else can duplicate the results. Ideally someone would do a bigger study, with thousands of participants. They would try to eliminate the noises and confusion, providing highly standardized conditions for testing. But who would do such research? And where? It would not be easy in rural Mozambique.

I'm impressed by Brown's research. It's a serious effort to test the miracle stories that come from Pemba, and it found scientifically credible results. Doubters, though, will have reasons to discount those results and remain doubters.

I'm more impressed by the community I saw at Pemba. Africans and Westerners work and live close together, in a simple, functional standard of living. Their lives are dedicated to helping the poor, not to glorifying Heidi and Rolland Baker. Miracles are not a show at Pemba; they are part of a unified ministry that focuses on Jesus.

Having been at Pemba, having heard many people from all backgrounds describe the miracles they have seen, I am convinced that God is using signs and wonders there to spread faith in Jesus Christ. There are just too many stories from too many sources who have little to gain from exaggeration. I don't expect that my belief will convince others, however. The miracles, I believe, are meant for those whose lives are affected, who live in Antonio's village and can verify that God has changed his life. The rest of us? We will need to see our own miracles, in God's own good time and place, and have faith in him even when we don't. As Jesus himself said, "Blessed are those who have not seen and yet have believed" (John 20:29).

In America, as in most of the West, Pentecostalism is an influential variety of Christianity, just one distinct flavor out of many. In the majority world, though, where most of today's Christians live, Pentecostalism has spread into virtually all churches, seasoning their worship, their teaching, and their hopes. It's not *an* influence; in many places it's virtually the Protestant church.

Some of the impact is merely stylistic. Pentecostalism is a way of shouting out prayers. It's a style of preaching. It's a particular flavor of music. It can even be a way of dressing or combing your hair. There's something deeper, however. Pentecostalism's power is not in organization or in style. It offers a chance to experience God.

Pentecostalism has led the way to a worship that is emotional and expressive. That unique achievement of Western civilization—to make music without moving your body—doesn't work with Pentecostalism. Shouting, dancing, singing, crying, raising hands high, kneeling low—in these and other ways, worshipers around the world express their love for God. Broadly speaking, that's an outflow of Pentecostalism.

Tongues are so important to Pentecostals because they experience it as the most basic (and wonderful) entry point to intimacy with God. They want everybody else to have the same experience.

What does this have to do with miracles? Only this: God and miracles go together. Seek God and you will find him doing wonderful things. When God walks the earth, the sick get healed. So it was with Jesus. So it is today.

But we go wrong when we show a higher interest in miracles than in God. This is Pentecostalism's persistent temptation—to let the effects of God's presence become more central than God himself. When God becomes mainly a miracle provider, he stops being God. He becomes more like a vending machine. Then pressure comes to provide more miracles, new miracles, unprecedented "phenomena" that stir excitement. Then "prosperity" becomes a formula rather than God's blessing given in a personal relationship.

In my experience, the core drive to love and worship God keeps Pentecostalism on track. However, you do find times and places where the manifestations of the Holy Spirit seem more important than the Holy Spirit himself—where people become more interested in miracles than in Jesus.

I'm thinking of meetings where only the most superficial gospel teaching is given, and the focus is almost exclusively on miracle healing. I'm thinking of groups that always seem to go on to "the next thing"—the latest manifestation of the Holy Spirit, whether laughing or prophetic utterances or dancing or trembling or singing or roaring. There's always something new to catch our attention, and the search for novelty becomes an addiction.

The so-called Prosperity Gospel is a classic case of how means get substituted for ends. God wants his people to prosper, and often he provides materially in a wonderful way—sometimes even in a miraculous way. The Prosperity Gospel, however, focuses on those provisions. In the Prosperity Gospel, wealth becomes the end, God the means to the end.

That is a danger in all faith: we want what God offers more than we want God himself.

Do Pentecostals see more miracles than other people? Miracles are not everyday occurrences anywhere. They are rare in India and Africa, too. Miracles sometimes break out in a spectacular shower, typically accompanying mass conversions of people with no background knowledge of God or the Bible. However, I know of nowhere that such showers of miracles have been a lasting pattern. You might call Mozambique an exception, but the revival is just fifteen years old. Will it continue with the next generation? I believe that miracles do happen more often in Pentecostal circles—because they ask for them more. They also look for them more, and more joyfully report them. Pentecostals have a view of God that urges them to ask. Those who ask, receive.

Most of the majority world prays freely for miracles—for healing, for exorcisms, for visions and words of knowledge. Most majority-world societies never stopped believing in the life of the spirit, so the Bible's worldview is not so hard to believe. Unlike the West, people in the majority world haven't had to get over the idea of nature as a machine.

The struggle is far from over, however. The West's dominance in science, education, medicine, and engineering practically guarantees that a materialistic worldview will carry on influencing people around the world. I foresee the materialist challenge growing as education increases. Pentecostalism could go one of two ways in response: it could become a Spirit-led rethinking and revaluing of learning, or a rejection of learning that makes the church into the refuge of an anti-intellectual, anti-scientific, poorly educated minority.

That leads us to the subject of our next chapter.

11

Can a Scientist Believe in Miracles?

It's all very good to talk of miracles in Mozambique. But we are modern people. We know the world operates according to impersonal laws. The sun rises and sets, people die or they live, and it has nothing to do with supernatural causes. Miracles belong to simple people who find it easy to believe. We know too much to be so gullible.

I feel a strong inward pull toward this point of view. When I first heard Sheri Moore announce her son Jeff's healing, part of me thought, *That's not real*. Either he was never truly injured in the first place, or else a psychological trick made him feel better (perhaps temporarily). Physical miracles—the rearrangement of bones—don't happen.

I think of Joby, who played on our church softball team. His wife was a Sunday school teacher, and he came to church only occasionally, when one of his children was singing. He liked softball, so we invited him to join the team.

At the beginning of the season we stood in a circle introducing ourselves. Most of the team mentioned what had drawn

165

them to our church. When Joby's turn came, he explained that he was Helen's husband, that he had a tremendous respect for her beliefs, but that he was an engineer, a very rational guy who couldn't believe in religion. He made it sound like an unfortunate fact of life: If you're rational, you are out of luck. You just can't get yourself in the faith mind-set; you can't make yourself believe what you know isn't true.

This point of view is often found among scientists and engineers. Oddly enough, it's not a scientific point of view. Science would seek to investigate. This position maintains that no investigation is necessary. We already know supernatural forces don't exist. Miracles don't happen. Religion is made up of beautiful myths and fantastic superstition.

This is a philosophical position—just the sort of philosophical *a priori* assumption that scientists say they abhor.

When I was in college, I took a class that talked about such philosophical issues. I particularly remember a thought experiment our professor offered. In the class we sat around a massive oak table. The prof asked how we would respond if one day during class, the table lifted up off the floor, hovered in the air for a few seconds, and then settled back down. How would we explain what had happened?

Some would call it a miracle. The hand of God had lifted the table, perhaps to send a message to us.

Some would insist on a physical explanation. Perhaps we had felt an earthquake. (We were, after all, in an earthquake zone.) Confused by the noise and the shaking of the quake, we might think that the table had hovered (though it hadn't).

Some would look for an explanation inside our heads. A mass delusion had occurred. Science might investigate the psychology of our delusion, not the table.

A great many of us might simply shrug and forget the incident. Nothing happened, nobody got hurt, it only lasted a few seconds. It was weird, but why worry about it?

Our class had an interesting discussion about worldviews and presuppositions influencing how we interpret events. But that couldn't prevent a more fundamental assault, coming from an engineer: "Why are we talking about this? Tables don't lift off the ground by themselves. It couldn't happen. It's entirely hypothetical!"

Not only do I identify with this reaction, I respect it. It's not a truly scientific response, but it's a commonsense one. When you hear a story that sounds like nonsense, it probably *is* nonsense. I feel the same way when I hear people talk about horoscopes, or conspiracy theories, or diseases healed by dietary supplements.

The problem is, while eliminating a lot of nonsense through such commonsense skepticism, you might also eliminate the one startling and important exception to the rule, something that opens up a door to new possibilities.

I'm thinking of Christopher Columbus, taking up the idea that you can find the East by sailing west.

I'm thinking of the first person to eat a tomato.

I'm thinking of the discovery that mosquitoes, not "bad air," carry malaria.

I'm thinking of the Wright Brothers, who flew despite having it proved to them that airplanes could never fly.

I'm thinking of the world-weary Roman leaders who put Jesus on trial—who couldn't shake off their certainty that Roman civilization was all that mattered, world without end, amen.

Many of the most significant findings of science begin with a counterintuitive idea, even a laughable idea. The geology of plate tectonics was discovered by a tiny minority of scientists who thought it possible that the rock under their feet was riding along the surface of the world like a boat drifting on water. Einstein made his earthshaking discoveries because he was willing to imagine that space could curve and that time could slow.

If you say that something could never happen, that it has to be nonsense, how did you find that out? How *would* you find that out?

In his book *Miracles*, C. S. Lewis takes on the materialistic understanding of the universe in which there is no "supernatural." Lewis understands that this is fundamentally a philosophical proposition. It sees everything tied together by cause and effect. If something happens, something physical must have caused it. Lewis calls this the "system." The materialist believes that everything can be explained as part of this web of causation—as mass and motion and energy. If you break it down to the basics, it's all physics. Why add imaginary forces, gods, spirits, or whatever? Stick with the simple explanation.

This is the mind-set that dismisses miracles as inconceivable. Since we can explain whatever happens through physics and chemistry and biology, there's no reason to toy with other explanations.

Lewis suggests that in two very important areas, though, the great web of cause and effect does not explain reality. It happens that the exceptions are crucial to science. In fact, science cannot exist without them.

One is reason. Reasoning is a mental operation by which a person—whether a scientist or not—arrives at truth. Through reason, facts lead to conclusions.

If we follow the materialist approach, the brain must be something like a computer, a collection of circuits that process electrical currents. Thoughts are what this brain computer produces. What we call reason must function through the brain machine, taking in facts and processing them to reach conclusions.

So who built the brain machine? Answer: nobody built it. The human brain was created by a long series of physical causes that caused it to emerge over millions of years. So how do we know that the machine gives correct answers? Might it not be that there is a built-in bias? Of course there might. The machine might be built to favor optimism, or to believe in ghosts, or *not* to believe in ghosts. The machine might automatically eliminate any answer that goes against its bias. We have no reason to believe the machine is unbiased.

There might be all kinds of reasons why the machine operates the way it does, with or without bias, but none of those reasons could possibly be truth. Truth is not a physical force that can build a machine. Nor can truth influence a machine.

In fact, truth stands independent of all influences and causes. Granted, we all have our biases, and we are all influenced by our circumstances. If I mention my bias, however, or the circumstances that affect my thinking, it is only because I want to deny that they have anything to do with my conclusion. Truth has to be independent of such factors if it is to be truth.

If I respond to someone's belief by saying, "You think that because you woke up on the wrong side of the bed," or "because your salary depends on you believing it," or "because you are temperamentally a pessimist," I have completely dismissed his thinking. Ideas that are based on such influences aren't to be confused with truth.

Socio-evolutionary theory is a good case in point. Materialists who take up this subject argue that every human behavior is caused by genes that want to multiply. If men prefer blue-eyed blondes, it's not that blue-eyed blondes are prettier, as the men think. Blue-eyed blondes must be more fertile than other types, and the genes, seeking to multiply, trick the brain into thinking that they are pretty.

If this is so, it also suggests that evolutionary biologists have genes telling them to spout evolutionary biological theories so they can mate more freely. It's not a matter of truth. It's a matter of reproduction. In either case, "beliefs" conceal what is really happening in the material realm.

If you are a rigorous materialist, you can't talk about truth. Truth has no material existence. But scientists talk about truth all the time. In fact, that is what science does: finds out the truth. Science can't be based on the proposition that believing a certain theory will help you mate more prodigiously. Do you think that sex drove the acceptance of Newton's theories about planetary orbits?

Somebody may argue that we don't know if reason produces truth, but we know that it works. There is a pragmatic evolutionary advantage to getting it right. But is there always? Isn't it sometimes advantageous to be falsely optimistic? Isn't it advantageous to love your family, even if it requires false ideas about whether they are good people? Isn't it sometimes advantageous to lie or trick others? Don't dogs sometimes growl when they are actually afraid?

At any rate, scientists don't talk as though they are simply pragmatists. When they describe the way the human cell operates, they give the strong impression that they are describing what actually exists, not just a collection of ideas they have found to generate workable results in their experiments so they can have a successful career and produce more offspring.

If there is only material cause and effect, truth is a figment of our imagination. Then we can never be sure of anything, even the proposition that cause and effect is all there is. Materialism refutes itself: you only say you are a materialist because you want to dominate me and win the argument and mate more often.

In a materialist universe, some physical cause is pushing our thoughts around. And that is an impossible situation for a scientist. Indeed, it is an impossible situation for anybody who wants to know the truth. If truth exists, it isn't created by material causes. It has an independent existence.

The second area that materialism can't account for is ethics—right and wrong. This is a particular subset of truth, and some people deny it really exists. Right and wrong are just people's opinion, they say, or just people's culture. They act as though right and wrong merely describe preferences, not values.

But scientists can't say that. The honesty of scientists is crucial. If they make up their data, if they invent observations, if the community of scientists is just a mass of striving, conniving careerists, how can science move on with any confidence it is getting at the truth?

Anyway, few people are willing to contend that kindness and caring for the earth aren't necessarily "right," or that treachery and deceit and murder aren't "wrong." But who says what are right and wrong? Where did those ideas of right and wrong come from? According to materialism, they must have come from some physical cause—certainly not from Truth or Goodness, which are not physical forces at all.

I find it a bit funny that the New Atheists are so passionate to prove there is no God. If they are right, who cares? And if they are right, how would we know? According to their own principles, it's just their genes talking, trying to "selfishly" dominate others, have more sex, and produce more children. Why on earth should we listen to them? But of course they can't honestly claim to be right. Materialism doesn't have space for right.

Science is not materialistic at all. It is a human endeavor that focuses on how things work at a mechanistic level. But science requires scientists, and scientists are not purely material forces. They are some kind of hybrid, physical animals who can reason their way to truth and must operate according to morality—neither of which can be understood fully by science.

The physical chemist Michael Polanyi made a great contribution to this understanding in his massive work *Personal Knowledge*. Starting with the most fundamental operations of science—measuring and counting—and working his way systematically through every facet of the discipline, Polanyi demonstrates that science doesn't work according to mechanical rules. There are always human factors—judgment, the recognition of patterns, and community, for example. A machine alone can never do science. Science requires persons. The knowledge it attains is personal knowledge.

So far, I haven't said anything about whether a scientist can believe in miracles. I've tried to show that a scientist can, and must, believe in things that aren't just cause and effect. Other factors operate in science, things like rationality and truth and right and wrong, which cannot come from a physical cause. They exist independently of physical causes. Perhaps a scientist can see that there is a crack opening up. What can fill the crack?

A friend of mine, Greg, tells a humorous story. He was working as a geothermal engineer in the Philippine head-quarters of a major energy company. Greg is a Christian who wanted to share his faith with his fellow employees. A crisis gave him an opportunity to do so, but not in the way he expected.

The problem came when two drilling rigs got stuck. Apparently this is a regular though dreaded problem when you are drilling holes thousands of feet below the surface of the earth. Something breaks, and you can't pull out the drill bit to fix whatever is broken. "The fish is in the hole" is how drilling engineers describe it.

Engineers have a basket of tricks to get the drilling rig out of the hole, but in this case, nothing they did worked. So they were deeply worried. The consequences were severe, even for a large energy company. It's quite possible that the entire drilling rig would have to be abandoned—that's millions of dollars of equipment—and a new hole started in a new location. This happening simultaneously in two different lo-cations would mean a huge hit to the company's profitability.

Greg's co-worker Tony was in charge of drilling opera-tions. Tony, like Greg, was a committed Christian, but with a significantly different style. Tony seemed clueless about respecting other people's religious sensibilities. He was ut-terly sincere, but not sensitive to how he came off to others.

Tony called a meeting at headquarters of all the key players. They went over the drilling problems and probed for solutions.

Everybody shared his expertise and experience, but no solutions were forthcoming. They had already tried everything. Finally Tony said, "We need to pray." He asked all the other employees—none of whom was known to be a believer—to kneel down and bow their heads while he prayed a passionate request that God would help them get the fish out of the hole.

My friend Greg was acutely embarrassed. He thought Tony's insensitivity would make him the butt of jokes for years to come. However, within a few hours of their meeting, word came from the drilling sites that both drilling rigs had been freed. They had come loose at approximately the same time that Tony led in prayer.

I'm not telling this story expecting to create belief in miracles. I tell it to raise the question, "What happened?" I mean, what physically happened? How exactly did those drilling rigs get free?

On one level, there's no miracle. Drilling rigs get stuck and drilling rigs come free, as unpredictably as getting your car out of a ditch by stepping on the gas. The miracle isn't the physical fact of the drilling rigs getting free, it is in the timing, in response to a very public prayer before a skeptical crowd. There is both a sign and a wonder in that.

But what happened physically? Did God send a tiny angel into the hole to move the rig? Did God's finger work it loose? Questions like this send the true believer and the skeptic flying apart in separate directions. The true believer may be quite happy to imagine tiny angels. The skeptic finds it impossible. "Miracles" he may be willing to contemplate as a broad, nebulous category. When you get specific, though, he breaks off and wants to quit. If miracles require belief in tiny angels, he will stick to skepticism.

I'm convinced this problem is based on a false conception, that nature and the supernatural are completely separate. We touched on this before. In one common way of thinking, the world is a finely tuned machine, and God must reach his finger in and adjust the machine occasionally. God was not at work in the deep recesses of the rock when the rigs got stuck in the hole, but he must have gone to work to free them—perhaps through a tiny angel sent in response to Tony's prayer.

This conception is wrong. God is always at work in the rocks. He holds them together. His smoothly unwinding handiwork is seen in everything—in rocks and trees and skies and seas. When we see a rose bloom, we are watching him sculpt using the materials at hand—his materials. There is nothing automatic about it: he does it again and again through the familiar ways (just as sculptors create statues using familiar tools), because they are the best ways.

If occasionally God does work in unexpected ways—for example, in releasing a drilling rig at the moment when a foolish but faithful servant of his puts his reputation on the line—he probably still does it with familiar tools. Vibrations or friction or whatever enables a rig to break free at any other time, he uses at the opportune time. Every miracle is physical and is done through physical processes, some of which we know and some of which we don't. God is there throughout. Physical processes are there throughout. But God is always the master: the artist, the physician, the engineer, the farmer.

I asked my friend Greg if he had experienced any other miracles. He paused and thought before saying yes, once. He had been tormented by bloody noses. For several years, he woke up every morning with a clot of blood on his pillow. He had tried whatever therapies were available without result. Finally one day, fed up with the sheer nuisance of it, he told God about his frustration and asked him to take the nosebleeds away. The next morning he woke up without a nosebleed, and he has never had one since.

Trivial? Yes. If you have asked for healing from a truly serious illness, this kind of story can be exasperating. Why would God choose to heal nosebleeds but not Parkinson's? I don't know.

The point I want to focus on is, What happened? If God healed Greg's nosebleed, did he alter his blood chemistry? Did he close up some capillaries? Could we find the evidence of tiny sutures?

My expectation is that God healed Greg's nosebleed through the way he normally does. You couldn't find evidence of abnormal activity, because it wasn't abnormal. It was normal. God is a healing God; he heals all the time. The timing may be a mystery, but the means really are not.

A few miracles—very, very few—seem to be completely abnormal: Jesus' turning water into wine, for example; Elijah's multiplying oil; Jesus' resurrection. Most miracles use ordinary, well-known processes, but the timing is extraordinary. Only these very rare miracles follow truly unusual pathways.

You rarely hear of such miracles. Macular degeneration may sometimes reverse, but amputated limbs don't regenerate. Can they? I don't see why not. In principle, the God who created the stars and the planets can grow extra body parts. He doesn't, however. He is not interested in that, I take it. He loves the normal ways of sculpting roses and healing diseases. He is the God of the normal, because the normal is his.

God does his miracles to stop us in wonder and to point toward himself. He does them physically, with the stuff he himself brought into being. He uses the ordinary forces, because they are his, too. If you look closely at a miracle, even the "abnormal," I don't think you will usually find anything that looks out of the ordinary. You will not find tiny sutures in the nose, nor will you accidentally X-ray the finger of God. God can do anything he wants, but he has his usual ways.

A crude analogy may help. At a bowling alley, what knocks down the pins? You may say that a bowling ball does. I prefer to blame the bowler. In reality, both are essential. But if I take a picture of the pins, it will be hard to see the bowler.

I hope I have helped the scientist see what fills the crack in reality—the crack opened up as we talked about reason and truth and right and wrong. That crack is filled with God. Is it so hard to believe that there is something before all stuff, that made all stuff, and that still activates all stuff? If you can believe in the Big Bang, why do you find it impossible and implausible to believe in God?

I want to say a word about the so-called new physics, since it has the potential for both helping and confusing the situation. In the nineteenth century, when many arguments about miracles became publicly prominent, people knew only the physics developed by Isaac Newton. This is generally the same physics you learn in high school today, with formulas that correlate mass, velocity, distance, and gravity. You learn to calculate the trajectory of a cannonball and other useful tricks. Such physics provided a model of the world that was orderly and predictable. It seemed that if you knew the details for every particle in the universe, you could predict everything that ever happened. The idea grew that miracles must violate the laws of nature, since they seemed to go against the stable predictability of Newtonian physics.

In the twentieth century, that all broke down, as scientists like Albert Einstein, Neils Bohr, and Werner Heisenberg discovered that reality was wilder and weirder than Newton had realized. In the world of the new physics, the observer affects the observation, time and space are flexible, and you locate a particle by calculations of probability, not certainty. To Newton, matter seemed to be solid, but now it has been revealed to be a cloud of dodging particles.

Some people thought this opened up the possibility of miracles. And indeed it did, if your mind had been closed by the idea that physical laws made the unusual illegal. But the enthusiastic optimism of some Christians regarding the new physics was misplaced, at least as far as miracles are concerned. For one thing, the wildness and the weirdness mainly related to infinitesimal particles at speeds near the speed of light. For events that a human being can observe without very special instruments, the new physics was irrelevant.

More to the point, the new physics, just like the old physics, was about the behavior of matter. It said nothing about its maker and sustainer. It said nothing about its purpose, nor even about its beauty. Physics new and old gives an elegant and important picture of the creation, but it offers only one view. And that view does not include the bowler.

The new physics does help in showing that the universe is not simple. Even Newton's universe was far from simple, but the universe revealed by the new physics teeters on the very edge of human understanding. "Common sense" does not tell you much about the world as it really is. Very rarified mathematics is needed to describe the world adequately—mathematics far beyond the grasp of most well-educated people, indeed most scientists. When you want to describe material reality in the most accurate way possible, you cannot speak English. It is not adequate. You have to speak mathematics.

And for those who can enter into that rarefied world, the world looks more strangely beautiful than ever. One reason why science is valuable is its revealing of the deeply complex and lovely structure of God's creation. Sadly, Christians have often been afraid of science, intimidated by the idea that its discoveries will undermine their faith. In reality, science reveals to us more of God's world.

That is not to say that science is incapable of mistakes, because it surely is. Science does, however, have a very good record of finding the truth about the material world. The airplanes we fly in and the telephones we talk on suggest how helpful its findings are.

Furthermore, rather than eliminating miracles, science can enhance our appreciation of them. It may be true that pre-scientific humans were more gullible about miracles. Since they did not understand the world's workings very well, they may have attributed ordinary events to miraculous causes. Solar eclipses, for example: we know that they are a predict-able result of the moon passing in front of the sun, while for prescientific humanity, they seemed to be divine warnings. Knowing how the world works, it's possible that we perceive fewer miracles than our ancestors did.

On the other hand, our attention may be sharpened. Take, for example, Jeff Moore, the boy in my church whose feet were healed. If there were no surgery, no medicine, no X rays and CT scans, we would only know that his feet hurt, and then they stopped hurting. Where is the miracle in that? But in Jeff's case, the power of medicine made his case all the more futile and frustrating, all the more dramatically out of human control, and thus all the more sharply wonderful when, at a word of prayer, he could suddenly walk again. Science enables us to see the world more clearly. As such, it debunks some miracles. It should, if it can. It also has the power to make us rejoice in the goodness of God's creation, and to marvel all the more at the exceptional works of power he sometimes does.

Can a scientist believe in miracles? He can, unless he has non-scientific blinders on. He can see all the more clearly.

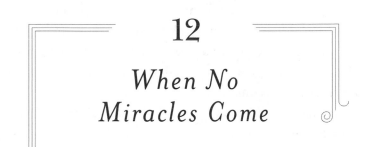

12

When No
Miracles Come

Just this week, as I write, Bill Slyker was buried. He was one of those from my church who followed Jeff Moore to Bethel Church, hoping to be healed of his fast-growing stomach cancer. He was not healed. But, as he told me, "Whether I live or I die, I feel like a winner." At his funeral, that statement was remembered many times by his family and friends.

Earlier this year, a good friend of mine, Nancy Sagherian, a missionary in Lebanon, went in for cancer surgery. The doctors had told her that she had two separate cancers in her abdomen, either one of which could kill her. Nancy's father is a man of deep and serene faith. He had been praying intensively from the moment he heard of his daughter's disease, and he was utterly confident. "He fully expected that when the doctors opened me up," Nancy told me, "they would find nothing—that all the cancers had disappeared." Instead they found that the cancers had spread so much that they could not operate.

Since then, Nancy has been in treatment with some success in shrinking the tumors. "I feel a great peace. [My husband] John and I are okay." They are most concerned with living out their faith through these difficult times. "The message we've given thousands of times to young people in Lebanon is, 'God is enough, God will take care of you.'" (With military invasions, vicious civil war, and economic devastation, Lebanese young people need to hear that message.) "Now we are living that out before the world."[1]

Another friend, Joanne Greenwald, died late last year after a long struggle against cancer. Joanne was a woman of deep faith—a lifetime schoolteacher who was deeply involved in missions around the world. I first met her in Kenya when she came to visit and impressed my wife and me with her deep curiosity, her desire to truly understand the challenges and joys of ministry in Africa.

During her illness, Joanne relied on a small army of friends to help her through multiple rounds of treatment. Joanne was a remarkable inspiration, maintaining great hopefulness that God would heal her and enable her to live on. She sent out emails to a long list of people who followed her progress, including me. Her treatment weaved its way through a series of threats, setbacks, special medical trials, and experimental approaches, each one extending her life. She was very aware of God's healing presence through them all. But the day came when treatments did not seem to be working. The cancer had metastasized once again.

Susan, a friend, took Joanne to get the results of her latest PET scan. As they walked to the waiting room, "Joanne took

1. Nancy did. As I was revising this book, she died, full of faith and thankfulness.

my arm and looked at me and said, 'Well, I'm nervous. This is a big meeting.' I looked at her and said, 'Well, "even if he does not . . ."' from Daniel 3. And we smiled at each other."

They referred to a passage from the Bible. Three young Israelites, their lives threatened by the Babylonian authorities, addressed the king: "O Nebuchadnezzar . . . if we are thrown into the blazing furnace, the God we serve is able to save us from it, and he will rescue us from your hand, O king. *But even if he does not,* we want you to know, O king, that we will not serve your gods or worship the image of gold you have set up" (Daniel 3:16–18 NIV, italics added).

There is no better verse to express faith under pressure. We know God can deliver us in any circumstances. But even if he does not, we will not change. We worship God alone.

Joanne died a month later.

In all these cases, my friends didn't get what they prayed for. Yet they weren't devastated. In fact, their faith continued strong.

Not everybody has such faith. The world is full of people puzzled, hurt, and angry that God failed to heal someone they loved and prayed for. People ask God for help in all kinds of situations: when they are in trouble with the law, when they face a big examination, when they're searching for work. Sometimes their prayers are answered, and they remember to thank God and grow in faith. Sometimes their prayers are answered, but when the crisis is over, they forget all about it. (Foxhole conversions aren't famous for having a lasting impact.) Much of the time, though, the answer to their prayers is no.

When Sheri Moore stood up in our church to announce that her son, Jeff, had been healed, I heard a smattering of cheers and "Praise God." My wife's voice was not among them. She was wary of celebrating.

In thirty-five years as a marriage and family therapist, she has helped more than a few people who believed strongly that God promised specific blessings to them, only to be let down. She is therefore slow to jump on the bandwagon when people proclaim God's deliverance. She knows that God helps people in wonderful ways, but she also knows that sometimes he doesn't do what people think he should. Often enough, no miracles come, and people are left disappointed, even bitter. She has seen it. She has helped people recover from it.

My friend Philip Yancey was a baby when his father contracted polio and died. Philip grew up without a father, though his mother often reminded him of the great Christian example his father had left behind.

Only as an adult did Philip learn the whole truth, after relatives shared some facts and he ultimately came across newspaper clippings. His father had been a highly visible example of faith healing. Christians all over Atlanta and beyond had prayed for him when they learned he had polio. When church leaders became convinced that God had answered their prayers, they celebrated and took him out of the hospital, removing him from the artificial lung that was helping him breathe. They did this so publicly that stories appeared in the newspaper, chronicling their faith. However, Philip's father died a few days later. He had not been healed.

Whether Philip's father would have died regardless, nobody knows. What's certain is that Philip grew up in an atmosphere of denial and hidden guilt. No one ever mentioned to him the circumstances of his father's death. I can only imagine the

effect on his mother—her loneliness compounded by her uncertainty about God's presence in that awful, scarring debacle.

Philip grew up denying the existence of God. Thankfully,
he was dramatically converted while in college. Not every
story has such a happy ending, however, and many times
I've met people who wrote off God because of a single bad
experience.

Bill Johnson, the pastor of Bethel Church where Jeff was
healed, has written a book on healing, *The Supernatural
Power of a Transformed Mind*. It is a thoughtful and biblical book about miracles, representing what I call the radical
charismatic movement. When these believers pray, they don't
take no for an answer.

Johnson asks,

> Aren't you tired of talking about a gospel of power, but never
> seeing it in action? Aren't you tired of trying to carry out the
> Great Commission without offering proof that the Kingdom
> works?
>
> God wants so much to invade this world with the reality
> of what was purchased on Calvary. But He waits for a people
> who will live the normal Christian life, putting themselves at
> risk, constantly tapping into the invisible resources of heaven
> that have been standing idle. . . .
>
> We have the exact authority Jesus has at the right hand of
> the Father. We are entitled and empowered to be His "House,"
> His embodiment on earth. As a Christian at this very moment,
> you have absolute liberty and access to heaven.[2]

2. Bill Johnson, *The Supernatural Power of a Transformed Mind* (Shippensburg,
PA: Destiny Image Publishers, 2005), Kindle edition, chap. 1.

My wife is cautious about miracle faith because of concern for the psychological and spiritual well-being of people who get disappointed. By contrast, Bill Johnson wants to throw caution to the wind.

Is there any way to do both? To be protective of fragile people, while at the same time bold and hopeful? How do we lean forward into the kingdom of God without losing our balance?

My friend and pastor Mike Griffin is a good example of both disappointment and reward in praying for miracles. When he and his wife, Beth, were newly married, they had a daughter, Kylie, who was severely disabled. Later, while Mike attended seminary, some charismatic Christian friends urged him to take his daughter to see Benny Hinn, an evangelist known for healing. Mike thought, *Why not? What do we have to lose?*

Mike and Beth took Kylie to a big event in Los Angeles. The atmosphere was intense and exciting. At one point the whole choir fell over in a faint when Hinn waved his arm over them. When Hinn invited people onstage for prayer, Mike and Beth didn't take Kylie up, but a small group of people gathered around her to pray for healing. Several of these praying people grew excited. They proclaimed that Kylie was healed. They were sure of it, thrilled by it.

Sadly, nothing really changed. Kylie was not helped by the experience, and the memories of it were painful to Mike and Beth. Their intense sadness over Kylie's disabilities was complicated by this experience. They realized that they *did* have something to lose.

A number of years later, Kylie died suddenly, and her loss was deeply sorrowful to Mike and Beth. Still bearing this hurt, they went into Beth's subsequent pregnancy with the hope that they would have another child.

Ten weeks into the pregnancy, Beth began to bleed profusely. Rushed to the hospital, she continued bleeding for two nights, and at one point her physician said she was virtually sure that Beth would lose the baby. Mike was in constant prayer. Standing or sitting by Beth all through the night, he had a very strong sense of God's presence, fighting for their baby's life. Each day when morning came, the hospital did an ultrasound and found that their child was still alive.

He stayed alive. Their son, Joshua, is alive and well as I write, a remarkably cheerful, energetic, and normal four-year-old who brings unbelievable joy to his parents. Mike says that night in the hospital room is an unforgettable memory of the miraculous presence of God.

As a pastor who's often asked to pray for people in their darkest times, Mike has reflected a great deal on these two experiences. In one case he was deeply, painfully disappointed. In the other, he believes God saved his son's life in response to his prayers. Mike writes:

> It reflects the dilemma presented in C. S. Lewis's classic, *The Problem of Pain*. If God has all the power available, if he can do anything, if he's infinitely loving, why wouldn't he want to answer my prayers for healing? It's a mystery. When someone is in the midst of suffering, as a pastor I can't necessarily help them with theological answers. I just have to stand with them in their sufferings.
>
> But when I look at what Scripture reveals, I think God's greatest concern is not healing but spiritual growth. He wants us to mature in our faith. And in my own life, I grew a lot

when God answered my prayers for Joshua, but I grew even more when God held me in my grief, when he didn't answer my prayers for Kylie in the way I had hoped. I deepened in my trust in God's faithfulness, and I grew more compassionate toward others. God knows what he is doing in each of our lives, and in each situation, though we may not understand it. One thing I can always know: he will use the experience in my life to grow my faith.

As a pastor, Mike says he wants to live *in* hope, not merely with hope. He encourages people to pray for miracles, and even to attend Benny-Hinn-type events if they feel called to. However, he suggests they attend along with people whom they trust and who will stick with them in the long run. Community helps people work through what can be very intense experiences, good and bad. Whether their prayers are answered as they hope or not, God wants to use whatever they experience for good.

Healing is part of the normal Christian life. God put it in His book; He illustrated it in the life of Jesus. He told us to emulate what Jesus did. So why is it so easy for us to be fully convinced when we pray for someone to be saved that our prayer will work, and yet when we pray for healing we find it difficult to believe they will be healed? Because salvation, as it pertains to a born-again experience, has been embraced and taught continuously by the Church for centuries, while the revelation of healing has not been widely embraced, and has even been fought. . . . Disease is considered a gift from God to make people better Christians! Think about how badly the Church has backslidden, to believe such lies! We have tolerated the deception that accuses God of doing evil, which is why today healing remains so controversial, little-practiced and little understood.[3]

That's Bill Johnson again. He goes on to speculate what the church would look like if healing had been embraced as "an essential part of the Great Commission. Normal Christians would see deformities and say, 'No problem.' Cancer, 'No problem.' Missing limbs, 'No problem.' We would pray in power without one iota of doubt."

As far as I know, there has never been a time or place in human history where people said, "Missing limbs, 'No problem.'" As Philip Yancey has noted, Lourdes displays discarded crutches and wheelchairs, but there are no glass eyes, no artificial limbs. And, I might add, no discarded coffins.

Why do Christians pray for salvation with confidence, but for healing with less confidence? Johnson is right that the church does that. But I don't think it's because of backsliding. I think the church teaches that because it deals with reality.

Many prayers for healing are not answered, and everybody dies eventually.

That is not how it is in heaven. But we're not in heaven yet.

Every single day we pray and hope for God to act "on earth as it is in heaven." And he often does. Most diseases are healed.

But we are only partway there. We await the fullness of the kingdom, when Jesus returns and heaven comes to earth "as a bride beautifully dressed for her husband" (Revelation 21:2). We live in the anticipation and frustration of "already, but not yet."

3. Ibid., chap. 4.

Johnson tells the story of a young man who fell and broke his arm at church. "I ran back and found him laid out on the ground, his arm clearly broken. I got down on the ground with him, put my hand on his arm, looked at the break—and suddenly fear stole into my mind. I forgot every miracle I had ever seen, and I said, 'Let's call the doctor.' "

Johnson says he wouldn't fault anyone for doing the same. "For most, it would be the proper thing to do."[4] But he clearly regrets that he thought of it himself—let alone acted on it.

Johnson wants to see only the kingdom of God. He acknowledges that his prayers aren't always answered as he thinks they should be, but his response is not to try to make space for this world's realism. Rather, he wants to keep leaning in to the possibilities of "on earth as it is in heaven."

Personally, I am going to call the doctor, and I won't feel guilty about it. I'll pray for a miracle, and I'll hope to see one, but my first responsibility is to care for that boy with the broken arm. I expect God to heal him through the normal, slow mending of the bone. That is not miraculous healing, but it is God's healing. The doctor's medicine is God's medicine.

Johnson wants my mind transformed so that my first and only impulse is to seek that miracle power. There's tremendous vitality in this Pentecostal mind-set. But I also see problems.

I see fellowships that live in denial. They believe in miracles, and they continually talk about those that occur. They don't much acknowledge the many situations where they don't.

4. Ibid., chap. 5.

They may end up with more hype than reality, which in the end makes people try to live as though they don't notice what actually goes on.

All the same, I see where Johnson is coming from. Who wants to be an expert in why God doesn't answer prayer? What's the value of telling people that they shouldn't expect too much when they pray?

Johnson is concerned, rightly, that when people talk about the kingdom as "already, not yet," they tend to drift toward "not yet." They stop living by faith. They don't live boldly and take risks.

Is there a way to live realistically in a world where miracles are rare, and yet still have a mind transformed by faith in God's power? How does one perform this balancing act?

"Once when I was ministering in Southern California," writes Johnson,

> a mother brought me a child who was tormented by devils. The child scratched and clawed at me while I prayed and bound and did what I knew to do—and yet my prayers had no apparent effect. The mother looked at me and said words I will never forget: "Isn't there anyone here who can help me?" Why did that mother bring that child to me? Because I represented someone—Jesus—who is absolutely perfect, knows no lack of power, and is absolutely willing to bring deliverance.[5]

Johnson asks whether we should conclude that it was God's will for the child to be tormented. No, he says, though that is the theology "many people embrace during times of uncertainty."

5. Ibid., chap. 8.

He concluded that he needed to spend more time in prayer and fasting, so that he had a reserve of deep intimacy with God. "My inability to bring the needed deliverance to the child has driven me to the throne. I must have more!" Then he would be able, like Jesus, to see heaven "erupt into the natural world at a moment's notice."

> We may find ourselves facing problems and not knowing where the tools are to bring about the solution. But that doesn't mean the problem is insurmountable. There is power in resolving in your heart that God is good all of the time, and that His will for healing and wholeness does not change, despite what we see in the natural.[6]

In his emphasis on prayer, I believe Johnson is absolutely right. The Father of Jesus Christ wants healing for all. He will bring it, not just for each one who seeks it in the name of Jesus, but for the whole universe. In the final outcome, healing is his will, always. Without bitterness, without resignation, we are to keep on praying and hoping for that. We may not understand why our prayers are ineffectual, but we should never draw the conclusion that the problem is meant to be permanent, or that God isn't interested in healing.

At the same time, I want to hold on to the words of Peter: "Dear friends, do not be surprised at the painful trial you are suffering, as though something strange were happening to you. But rejoice that you participate in the sufferings of Christ . . ." (1 Peter 4:12–13 NIV).

"But do not forget this one thing, dear friends: With the Lord a day is like a thousand years, and a thousand years

6. Ibid., chap. 8.

are like a day. The Lord is not slow in keeping his promise, as some understand slowness. Instead he is patient with you, not wanting anyone to perish, but everyone to come to repentance" (2 Peter 3:8–9).

We should never lose sight of the kingdom, and we should always pray fervently and hopefully for God to do "on earth as it is in heaven." But we should also be patient and remember that God can do a great deal of good as he guides us through the painful (and slow, by our accounting) renewal of his creation. We should never spread blame on others or on ourselves when miracles don't happen as we want them to.

God is really in control. He wants us to pray, but he does not depend on us working ourselves into a state of "faith." He has his own timing. Miracles are not hard for him, but he is most concerned with character and love, which can and do grow in times of perplexity and strain.

My friend Tim Hostetler became a Christian in the California Jesus movement.

At the age of twenty-one, I was a new Christian and I badly needed $20 to pay a bill. I remember getting down on my knees and asking God to somehow provide me with that money. I went to my mailbox, and there was a letter from someone I didn't know, with a check for $20.

I later found out that two weeks earlier, my sister had been talking to a lady who said she liked to send out checks to people in need. My sister told her that I probably needed some money, and she wrote me a check. When I learned about it I was amazed that God was not constrained by time. He put the answer to my prayer in motion two weeks before I prayed. There was no limit to what he could do in answering our prayers.

Lots of people have miraculous experiences like that when they are new Christians. Like little children when they pray, they see God's answers in direct and beautiful ways.

Forty years later, Tim still knows that God has no limits, but he also knows that God does not always answer our prayers as we want. Tim has prayed for many people who were healed, yet he himself has suffered from chronic illness—disabling back pain, terrible digestive pain, regular migraine headaches. He's been on disability for decades. He's visited every doctor possible, and Christians all over the state have prayed for him. He's still very sick.

"I've had thousands of migraine headaches, and I've had people pray for me hundreds of times. Only once have I been healed, when a man put his hand on my head and the pain went away immediately. I started praying for the research people in the labs. Since God wasn't healing my migraines through prayer, I thought medicine might be the way. And I thank God for Imitrex, because it really helps."

Tim quotes Corrie ten Boom, walking in warm sunshine in the beautiful Southern California hills. "Isn't God good?" asked a friend who was walking alongside. Answered Corrie: "God was good in Ravensbruck."

Her sister died in Ravensbruck, a Nazi concentration camp. She suffered unimaginably. Why? Surely not because God wants to see us suffer. Surely not because Corrie ten Boom lacked faith. We don't know why, and the Bible doesn't say. What we know is that God is good and brings good out of evil. He may do it through miraculous deliverance, but he also may do it through the transformation of character that occurs when we suffer.

Sometimes God shows his goodness by piling on benefits for all to see. Other times he does it by letting us suffer—as Jesus himself suffered—in order that others might see the power of God in our faithful endurance. He did it that way in the life of Corrie ten Boom. He's done it in the life of my friend Tim.

I've lately been struck by short, little-regarded Psalm 67. It begins with a classic, generic prayer:

> May God be gracious to us and bless us
> And make his face shine upon us.

All the basics are in that prayer: a longing for God's gracious forgiveness, for his blessing, and for a sense of his shining, personal presence. That's what I pray for when I don't know what to pray, when I'm lonely or discouraged or confused. "God bless us." We pray this way when we need a miracle. "God bless us."

We are naturally selfish when we pray, as this psalm shows. "Be gracious to US and bless US and shine upon US." We pray for others, but we pray most fervently and spontaneously for ourselves. I may pray for your children, but not as much as I pray for mine.

What makes the psalm so magnificent is what comes next:

> So that your ways may be known on earth,
> your salvation among all nations.

The Israelites were not particularly famous for thinking of other tribes. They were a tiny nation surrounded by enemies, and their thinking more often went: "God bless us and defeat our enemies." In this psalm, however, another view leaks out. "Bless us so that our enemies will see and know what kind of God you are—gracious and full of blessing." The prayer goes on:

> May the peoples praise you, God;
> may all the peoples praise you.
> May the nations be glad and sing for joy. . . .

The psalmist is not content for the surrounding nations to see God's goodness to Israel. He wants them to *praise*. He asks for gladness and joy to spread to them. He pictures blessing extending to the ends of the earth, leading to praise and delight in God's good and just reign. The whole world will sing for joy together.

This vision was not new to the psalmist. God's call to Abraham (Genesis 12:1–3) contains the same dynamic, "blessed to be a blessing." Our fundamental motive when we pray for miracles should be that our blessing might lead others to join the joyful parade.

In the New Testament, another dimension enters. The believer can bless the world as he or she suffers. Jesus showed the way. From his suffering and death comes a new, loving community of people, open to anybody who has faith in God. Blessing spreads joy, but suffering also spreads joy, as the Christian's character shows through.

God's power does mighty miracles throughout the New Testament, but those same Scriptures spend most of their energy telling us how to live together and love each other. Those are our most powerful witnesses before a watching world.

We need to set our hearts on those matters that God cares most deeply about. One day he will come and reward our faith, and all manner of sickness and trouble will be healed forever. Then, miracles will be normal, "on earth as it is in heaven," because the two have merged.

13

What We Know and How We Should Use It

We have been on a lengthy journey through the Bible and church history, philosophy and science, experiences with miracles and without them. I think it is worth summing up what we have learned.

Here are twenty simple affirmations we can make about miracles:

1. God is the master of everything that happens, whether we call it miracle or not. We should praise God for his work in healing by medicine and in healing by miracle. We should praise God for miraculous signs and for non-miraculous sunsets.

2. The distinction between miracle and non-miracle mainly has to do with surprise. Miracles are when God walks on unusual paths, to our wonder.

3. Miracles happen. Reliable people testify to miracles. As with all historical events, trustworthy witness is the only real test.

4. Miracles are signs and wonders. They are not violations of God's natural order, but signs of his unusual activity within that order. They are meant to seize our attention.

5. Signs do not draw attention to themselves, but to something else.

6. Miracles are signs pointing toward resurrection. Jesus did miracles that prefigured his resurrection. Our miracles are a foretaste of our resurrection, and of the renewal of the whole earth.

7. Miracles are symptoms and signs of God's kingdom, but not the substance. The substance is Christ. We should focus our faith and hope on him.

8. Miracles are rare; otherwise they would not be miracles.

9. Healings are common. God has made a healing universe. Only rarely does healing surprise us so much that we call it a miracle.

10. The fullness of the kingdom is not yet here. We are waiting for Jesus to return and set everything right. So miracles remain rare until Jesus comes. (In some places and times, they may come in clusters, but the clustering is only for a time.)

11. Miracles are not a proof of genuine faith, nor is their absence a proof that something is wrong with our faith. Some of the most faithful people in the Bible saw no miracles; some of the least faithful saw many.

12. Miracles are signs pointing to the kingdom, but so is righteous suffering.

13. Miracles usually make an impact on a small number of people who witness them firsthand. That is how it was with Jesus, and it is usually so today.

14. People like to pass along miracle stories uncritically, so many of them don't hold up to scrutiny. But that doesn't mean that none are true.

15. Miracles happen in messy circumstances—not necessarily in holiness and radiant light, but often in confusion among people with deep problems.

16. For long centuries, in both biblical history and in the generations since Jesus, few or no miracles were recorded. We don't know why; it certainly does not seem to be a result of human unfaithfulness. God's work continued, and his presence was real despite the lack of miracles observed.

17. The Bible doesn't tell how to do miracles. Jesus used so many different techniques that there's little guidance to be had in studying his methods. Technique isn't the issue. Miracles come out of a relationship with the living God.

18. Physical miracles—healings, most prominently—can be described through physical processes. Just because you can explain how something happened medically or scientifically doesn't make it any less miraculous. Everything that happens is natural and supernatural at the same time.

19. God's greatest concern is that your faith grow—whether through miracles or not.

20. God will heal everybody—the whole world—when his kingdom comes in all its fullness. Miracles signal that coming day.

These twenty terse statements summarize what we have learned. I hope they shed some light. The point of my writing isn't simply to understand miracles, though. I also want to offer guidance in the way we live. Here are some principles to hold on to as you walk through life with a God of miracles.

Keep your eyes wide open to see God at work.

A key part of every Christian's job description is *witness,* which begins with seeing.

Most of what God does is ordinary. The sun rises every day. Families love each other every day, too. Birds sing, crops grow, mathematicians theorize. And God is at work in all these things: the inspirer, the activator, the power. He is never absent and always active. Keep your eyes open to such ordinary things and learn to see God's power in them. This will help you avoid the false idea that miracles occur when God's power switch is "on," while the absence of miracles means that his power switch is "off." It is always on. He has never stopped working, not for one second. Christians should be witnesses of that.

Keep your eyes open to seeing new things.

For all that God does in ordinary ways, we know that God sometimes does the extraordinary and surprising. How do we know? He did it in Jesus. And since Jesus is alive today, we should keep our eyes open and our minds alert to see new and amazing things.

Hope to see God do miracles.

We should do more than be open-minded and open-eyed. We should hope.

We hope because we know what God can do. When we read the Bible, we learn of unthinkable wonders he has done. We hope to see them for ourselves, prefiguring the fullness of the kingdom of God.

Pray for what you want and need.

We play an active role in miracles: we pray. If someone is sick, we pray for healing. If someone is desperate, we pray for God's miraculous provision. We ask, and we keep on asking.

This, above all, is how we show our faith. It's not a magical frame of mind, a blind belief-in-spite-of-reality. It's prayer that's persistent, simple, and from the heart.

Pray for God's will above all else.

Jesus set the ultimate model when he prayed in the Garden of Gethsemane. "My Father, if it is not possible for this cup to be taken away unless I drink it, may your will be done" (Matthew 26:42). That's the very definition of Christlike behavior.

Some say that healing is always in God's will. True, but we don't know God's timing. God will heal everyone in his new world. We aren't there yet.

When you hear of a miracle, thank God.

Not every report is genuine, but you are not the miracle police. Thank God for what you hear. "Rejoice with those who rejoice" (Romans 12:15).

Don't spread the word unless you have firsthand knowledge.

If you have firsthand knowledge of something marvelous God has done, by all means pass on the word. That's witness. Don't, however, join in miracle gossip. It's not helpful.

It seems innocent to pass on reports you've heard about miracles, but many of those reports give a false impression that undermines gospel credibility when the truth comes out.

Sustain spiritual disciplines to guard your heart and mind.

Because miracles are rare, hope can lead to cruel disappointment. We need spiritual disciplines to sustain us. We read the Bible. We worship with other Christians. We fellowship with other believers. We pray. Our spiritual disciplines keep us in the habit of hoping, and they protect us from discouragement.

Don't test God.

Testing comes when people have seen God's faithfulness but keep asking for more proof. The classic example came at a place called by two names in Scripture: Massah, a Hebrew word which translates as "testing," and Meribah, which translates as "quarreling."

On their way from Egypt to Palestine, the people of Israel grumbled about Moses' leadership. Hearing their complaint, God provided water through a miracle. I expect the Israelites felt very holy when that happened.

Scripture makes it abundantly clear, however, that God was not happy. They had been unwilling to wait to see how God would provide; they demanded an immediate response on their terms. Psalm 95:8 warns Israel never to repeat the performance. (This was the Scripture Jesus quoted when Satan suggested he jump off the temple and have God rescue him.)

God is looking for people who trust him, not people who test him.

Don't think miracles depend on you using the right words, thinking the right thoughts, or praying with the right technique.

There are no magic words. Jesus made this extremely clear when he taught his disciples on the subject of prayer. (See Matthew 6:5–13.) He told them to pray quietly, using few words rather than many.

We often want something more complicated. Sometimes it is the tone of voice—an emphatic "in the name of *Jesus*!" Or it could be a verbal formula: "Satan, I bind you!" or, "We stand before you in the power of the Holy Spirit." Some suggest that we should address the trouble directly: "I command this leg to heal!"

These may be mostly harmless, but they can lead us into a false understanding of God's character. He cannot be talked into doing what we want by our clever approaches. What kind of God would stand back, denying us his wonderful benefits because we didn't get the phrasing right?

Pray for each other.

The New Testament examples of miracles show one person helping others. A woman who couldn't stop bleeding reached out to Jesus and touched him, and thus was healed. A Roman centurion sent messengers to Jesus asking him to come; his servant was healed. Peter and John saw a lonely beggar at the temple gate, and told him to stand up. Through the help of a faith-filled person, all these were healed. We are not isolated individuals. We need each other.

Don't judge other people's faith, or the lack of it.

"Who are you to judge someone else's servant?" (Romans 14:4).

Before you pray for someone, ask permission.

Praying for others in person is a deeply intimate act. People who need prayer are very vulnerable.

Make sure you understand their concern. (One easily jumps to conclusions.) Listen carefully, then repeat back in your own words what they are concerned for. If there's any doubt, get them to say it again.

If you want to put a hand on them as you pray, ask if that's okay, and tell them where the hand will go. If the prayer will be long, warn them. If you will ask them to pray out loud for themselves, ask whether they want to do that. If other people are joining you in prayer, introduce them. If you will pray in tongues, say so and ask permission. If there might be shouting, let everyone know and ask whether that is okay. The object is to make everyone feel safe.

Ask gifted people for help.

Some people have special gifts for healing or miracles. (See 1 Corinthians 12:7–11.) When someone has been identified with these gifts, you surely want to ask their help.

Avoid celebrity cults.

As Paul makes extremely clear in the rest of 1 Corinthians 12, no one person with particular gifts should be singled out for more honor than anybody else.

Seek miracles in community.

You're emotionally and spiritually vulnerable when you seek miracles. Community is a very helpful antidote. Don't pray alone; pray with people you trust. Don't go to a healing meeting alone; go with others who know you, who will help you with discernment, and who will be with you for the long haul.

Avoid fellowships that make you feel guilty.

Watch out for the groups that suggest, subtly or not, that the reason you don't see miracles is your lack of faith. You didn't try enough, you didn't believe enough, or you didn't give enough money. We call that "works" religion.

Avoid fellowships that can't or won't talk about suffering, pain, or sickness.

Suffering, pain, and sickness are part of the human condition. John Wimber once told me that the people in his church might be sicker than average, because sick people were drawn in. That's the atmosphere to look for. Think of Jesus. Weren't his crowds full of needs? Weren't his disciples?

Look for the bigger meaning of signs and wonders.

Signs and wonders point to something bigger than themselves. They often accompany a vast outbreak of faith, as in China, India, and Africa today. God uses miracles to make people stop and listen. So listen!

Live in hope.

When you live in hope, it's not just a plea for God to fix one troubling piece of your life—your sickness, for example. God will transform everything—all of you and all the world. It's a full-body, full-mind, full-planet, full-cosmos hope. God wants to make *all* things new, not just you.

We hope for God's revolutionary transformation of the universe, his healing of all wounds, his abolition of sighing and sadness. Hope cannot be centered just in my ambitions; it has to find its shape within God's great plans.

God is who he says he is, the God of great power and grace who has sent his Son to save us. We rejoice in the knowledge that he is a miracle God. We rejoice in the hope that he will do as he has promised and set us all free.

14

Last Words

Bethel Church, where Jeff Moore was healed, is a big-box megachurch perched on a hilltop in Redding, California. When I visited, the surrounding mountains were covered in snow. It was beautiful.

Though Redding is far off the beaten track, people come from all over for the Bethel experience. The church offers a striking atmosphere, warm and full of excited anticipation. At the Friday evening worship service, two women painted semi-abstract canvases from the stage while the music, prayers, and preaching went on. The band played a kind of U2, wall-of-sound style while a tall blonde woman stood by with a hand raised over them like the angel Gabriel. Was she praying for them? Protecting them? Nobody said.

It's hard to say on the basis of one visit whether miracles are at the center of the Bethel experience, but they certainly aren't far off. Even though the sermon had to do with the creativity and excellence needed by the people of God doing kingdom work, the preacher told several dramatic healing stories, including one in which he helped a woman in Michigan get publicly healed of multiple ailments, including having amputated toes grow back. After he prayed for her feet, he said, he had her take off her shoes and count her toes. Voilà! Ten toes! The congregation cheered and laughed when he told this story.

After the service, ministry team members lined the front of the auditorium. So many in the congregation sought healing or other helping prayers that many of us had to wait for our turn.

I went forward, asking for prayers for vision. Six months before, I suffered a detached retina, and the vision in my left eye was fuzzy. It wasn't a devastating problem—my right eye compensated—but I would have loved to see properly from both eyes. A young man from Croatia who attends Bethel's School of Supernatural Ministry prayed for me three times. Unfortunately, my eyesight remained fuzzy.

I don't know whether others were healed that evening. Three people were lying on the floor by the time I left, but no miracles were announced.

The next morning I attended Bethel's Healing Rooms, a Saturday-morning ministry. About fifty of us sat in a large lounge with subdued lighting, waiting our turn for prayer. A band played worship music, two painters worked on canvases, and several young women did expressive dancing all around the room. Our leader at one point announced, "Does anybody here have a headache? God is healing headaches right now." A middle-aged woman approached him, he touched her, and she began spasmodic movements with her hands and head. "Good-bye, headache!" the leader said cheerfully while the woman was helped to the floor, where she lay undisturbed for the next thirty minutes.

A few minutes later a word of knowledge was announced: Someone had severe pain in the left jaw. We waited, but nobody owned up to it.

While I waited my turn to go into the healing rooms, the leader announced that in one of the first groups, a man had a toothache healed. The leader also said that telephone counselors who use Skype to pray for people seeking healing had heard from a woman with schizophrenia. They had prayed for her last week, and this week she called back to say that she was totally healed. She had been on an even keel all week, she reported, and she had stopped taking her medicine.

A cheer went up, but I was alarmed. Anybody who works with the mentally ill knows that they are prone to delusions, including the delusion of being healed. The first thing they do is quit their medications, a choice that can cause devastating damage to their brains. I can only guess that the Bethel training does not include information about mental illness. I was reminded that ministry is not a risk-free business. Real harm can be done. I hope and pray that the schizophrenic woman really was healed rather than suffering from delusions.

After forty minutes of waiting, I was called into another large room, where two friendly and caring people prayed for my eye. I wasn't healed. Those who prayed for me didn't pressure me in any way, and although they were obviously disappointed that my vision was not healed, they didn't suggest a lack of faith or other deficits in me. Rather, after trying to heal me several times, they prayed a prayer of blessing over me and let me go.[1] All told, I was there about an hour.

I didn't see any miracles, though several people were lying on the floor and might well have been healed or helped by prayer.

Bethel's website has a "good news" section, which shares news of healing miracles. Those posted as I write this, a few days after my visit, have to do with a heart murmur disappearing (I heard this testimony given verbally), an unspecified cancer healed, allergies disappearing, a slipped disc improved, rheumatoid arthritis alleviated, and a sore ankle improved. In no case is there any mention of doctors, nor are medical details provided. (The testimony about the heart murmur seems to confuse a heart murmur with an irregular heartbeat.)

I know for a fact that people are miraculously healed at Bethel. Jeff Moore was. But it's worth noting that these Bethel healings were predominately "soft." Allergies, back conditions, joint pain, and arthritis all change day to day. Their healing means a lot to the people directly involved, but it's not likely to impress outsiders. You can find similar healings at conferences dedicated to organic foods or alternative medicine.

I got the feeling that people at Bethel don't worry about such matters. They are utterly enthusiastic and unquestioning about the amazing things that God is doing in their midst. They don't seek to verify miracle stories because they don't see the point. God is doing wonderful works, and they only want to celebrate.

1. Ultimately I was healed, however, through cataract surgery. I thank God for that!

Take the woman with the amputated, regrown toes. If that really happened, it wouldn't be hard to document it. Surgeons who amputate toes keep detailed records. I'd like to have proof that it really happened. But as far as I could see, there was no curiosity about that. She said it had happened; praise the Lord.

I very much appreciated Bethel's warmth and welcoming spirit, the cheerfulness and the lack of public hype. I liked their sense of excited anticipation. It reminded me very much of John Wimber's Vineyard church when I visited there twenty-five years before.

The Vineyard later experienced growing pains. The intoxicating excitement of the early days gradually got tempered by experience. Some people were healed; a lot were not. Healings of shortened legs or bad backs grew less exciting as time went on; so did seeing people fall down and twitch. The Vineyard had to find its way to a ministry that centered on the gospel with healing as part of the whole. Along that journey, the church took some strange and painful side trips into Pentecostal excess. From my view as an outsider, they came through safely. Today I see them as a solid charismatic denomination with a strong gospel ministry.

My guess is that if Bethel is intoxicated with miracles, it will be tempered by experience just as The Vineyard was.

That's not their expectation. They believe God is doing something new, that they are on the front of a tsunami that will change everything. They see miracles increasing and spreading everywhere, becoming normal, not rare.

I don't see much evidence that such expectations are correct, either biblically or sociologically. But God is full of surprises, and if they are right, I'm for it! Whether a tsunami of miracles comes, or more of the up-and-down struggle that has been the common experience of Christians through the ages, we still need to center on the gospel. We still need to exhibit patience and faithfulness through all kinds of suffering until Jesus comes. Those are gospel facts.

As I reflect on Bethel, I'm grateful that they prayed for Jeff Moore—and for Tom Bryant and Bill Slyker, who weren't healed. I don't see my church becoming like Bethel, but I do think we can learn from them.

At my church, you can come forward for prayer every Sunday. Besides that, any day of the week somebody asking for prayer gets prayed for by pastors and other church members. Just two weeks ago I joined a prayer team in praying for a suffering neighbor.

I wonder, though, how clearly we proclaim our faith in a miracle God. I wonder if we lean into the kingdom of God, looking for signs and wonders. I wonder if we tell the story of Jesus with enough emphasis on his miraculous powers.

I talked to Jeff Moore today. He's working at a machine shop and exploring other career options. He sounds happy. It's been nearly four years since his healing.

"I don't talk about it as much as when it first happened," Jeff told me.

> Everybody then knew I was in a wheelchair, so they could see the change. Now it doesn't come up as often.
>
> I'll tell some people about what happened and I can tell they aren't impressed. They probably don't believe me. I still think about it a lot. It still feels strange to me. Why did God decide to heal me as opposed to others?

I talk with my dad about it the most. We'll be discussing some memory and realize I was in a wheelchair at that time. I'm still amazed at what happened, and grateful.

I talked to Jeff's father, Bob. He expressed similar feelings: amazement that Jeff had been healed, and regret that the wonder of it has dimmed as time passed.

"When Jeff was first healed, Sheri wrote the date on our whiteboard. Next to that she wrote, 'All is well.' It's still there. Sometimes I look at it and think back to that time. Whenever we are struggling with something hard, I'll remember Jeff's experience and tell myself, 'This isn't so hard.' "

I wish that leaders in our church had offered to pray for Jeff to be healed. Jeff always had that option, but I think it would have been better if someone who knew him had directly offered it to him. I wish we had been thinking that way, knowing that our God does miracles.

I wish that we had celebrated more when Jeff was healed, rather than taking a cautious, wait-and-see response.

I don't want to be too self-critical, though. On the good side, we offered what Jeff and his family most needed. We were their church family. People knew them and cared for them and worshiped Jesus with them. Four years later, we still know them and care for them and worship with them. If our church has been weak on miracles, we're strong on what matters most, the death, resurrection, and eternal kingdom of Jesus.

I remember preaching once in a village in India. One of the embarrassing things that happens when you travel to remote parts of the world is this: they ask you to preach.

They themselves are much better qualified, knowing the language, the culture, and the people's needs. Besides, they are probably holier people than you. And in my case, they are almost certainly better preachers. Nevertheless, you can't easily say no—it wouldn't be understood. So I preached.

The church had been started by a young Pentecostal man who moved into the area as an engineer for the utility company. Finding no church to worship in, he launched a meeting in his home. When he witnessed to some local prostitutes, the congregation began to grow. Then his wife gave birth to premature twins who seemed destined to die. He fasted and prayed for three days, and the children survived. Word spread, and more people came to church.

Several times fundamentalist Hindu mobs attacked the church, threatening people and burning Bibles, and once, the police arrested the pastor and threatened him. He kept on. The result was a congregation of well over one hundred people meeting in a newly plastered, open-air structure nearly devoid of furniture. People sat on woven mats, women on the left, men on the right. The air was close with body heat and perspiration. Earsplitting singing vibrated the building to the accompaniment of drums.

My sermon was presented via translation. Having little idea what was relevant to my audience, I stuck close to my Bible text. The congregation listened closely, though I had no idea what penetrated.

After the service people besieged me, asking for prayer. So many crowded around me that I got backed into a corner and could not move. I remembered Jesus, tugged at and crowded by the mobs seeking healing.

My translator told me the request of each person, and I laid hands on their heads or held their calloused hands while I prayed. Some were sick, some needed work, some wanted husbands to return home. They were oppressed by spirits, worried about pending school exams, or had family disputes. One complaint I did not immediately understand: "She has Fitz," my translator said. "What?" I asked. "Fitz," he said again. "You know, Fitz! Fitz!" It dawned on me: the lady had fits. Epilepsy. I prayed for her.

I don't know what happened as a result of those prayers. I saw no visible changes. I left that village and never saw it again. Perhaps miracles came. Perhaps the woman with epilepsy was healed. Perhaps not. I will probably never know.

Truthfully, I don't think it's the most important thing. Of course I would love to see my prayers answered miraculously, and I would love to know that those people were healed or helped in surprising ways. But I care much more that the church is still on that spot, still witnessing to the gospel of Jesus Christ. The power for that village lies there—in the Good News believed and proclaimed.

In my personal prayers, I often use the Lord's Prayer. I find it a helpful template as I pray through all kinds of issues. Jesus taught us to pray this, so it has to be right.

The Lord's Prayer centers on the most basic stuff of the kingdom. It starts with the request that God's reputation be set apart, his name above all other names. This comes first: God's reputation.

Then we pray that God's kingdom come, "on earth as it is in heaven." As I noted earlier, every time we pray this prayer, we pray for miracles. But not only for miracles. Also for peace. For justice. For love. For exploited, war-weary, hungry, and lonely people, we pray that God's kingdom come on this earth.

We pray for what we need: daily bread, forgiveness, protection from evil.

And then we close: *for yours is the kingdom, and the power, and the glory forever. Amen.*

For many years I took this as a throwaway line. Now I see its deep significance. Lest our prayers get carried away in the wrong direction, this closing prayer sets us straight.

Yours is the kingdom. I have learned to add, in a small voice, "Not mine." God's plans and his governing power are at stake. My plans and my powers don't matter too much in comparison. It's easy to lose that perspective when we pray for miracles. We very easily begin building up our plans and our program. But humbly we should acknowledge: yours is the kingdom.

Yours is the power. Also not mine. When we pray for miracles, we very easily think it depends on us. But this clause reminds us that only God does miracles. He alone has power.

Yours is the glory. Miracles are glorious, but the glory is all God's and not mine at all. If I seek my own glory in any way, I go off course.

Miracles are wonderful gifts from God, but they also bring temptations. Satan knew that when he tempted Jesus, offering him the chance to do miracles. Jesus passed the test by *not* doing miracles, because that was not what God had called him to do at that moment.

We are tempted to seek kingdom, power, and glory for ourselves. But not even Jesus would take them for himself. To

God only belong the kingdom and the power and the glory. He is the miracle worker.

It is in God's very nature to astonish us by his goodness. He does wonders as he wishes, in complete freedom. And we—we ask. We watch. We witness and express our grateful thanks.

Tim Stafford is a lifelong professional writer, with more than twenty published books, two of which have won Gold Medallion awards. Tim serves as senior writer for *Christianity Today* magazine and has published hundreds of articles in that and other publications. He lives with his wife, Popie, in Santa Rosa, California.